Connecticut:

The Provisions State

By CHESTER McARTHUR DESTLER

A Publication of
The American Revolution Bicentennial
Commission of Connecticut

Published by

PEQUOT PRESS

Chester, Connecticut

1973

ISBN: 87106–122–8
Library of Congress Catalog Card Number: 73–83249
Manufactured in the United States of America
All Rights Reserved
FIRST PRINTING

Contents

Illustrations

Connecticut: The Provisions State

Each of the fifty states has its nickname, and some of them have several. Connecticut, to its credit or discredit, can boast of three. To some, Connecticut is known as "The Constitution State," a name which is applied because the colony's "Fundamental Orders" of 1638 is sometimes described as the first written constitution in the English-speaking world. Others know Connecticut as "The Nutmeg State," a sobriquet much less flattering, since it derives from the Yankee peddlers' alleged selling hand-carved, wooden, counterfeit nutmegs to unsuspecting customers in back-country villages and farms to the south and west. Of these two oft-used names, the one is based upon a questionable historical assumption, and the other is pure fiction. Much more complimentary, and certainly more accurate, is "The Provisions State," for such, indeed, Connecticut truly was during the American Revolution.

An older generation of Connecticut historians stoutly maintained that throughout the colonial period, Connecticut agriculture was an exceedingly primitive one of the "subsistence" type, and that it yielded only a poor, self-sufficing life for the farm families which in 1775 constituted nearly ninety per cent of the population. More recent studies, however, particularly those of Gaspare John Saladino, Albert E. Van Dusen, and Richard L. Bushman (see Bibliographical Note), have effectively demonstrated that mid-eighteenth century Connecticut agriculture was not the "hard-scrabble" operation it is sometimes assumed to have been. Certainly a mere "subsistence" agriculture would have been incapable of such a sudden expansion in 1775 as to provide a surplus large enough thereafter to feed its militia and much of the Continental army, provide produce to export in return for arms and powder, supply the colony's armed vessels, and provision the many privateers that harassed British shipping off the New England shore. Yet, during 1776–1783, it accomplished all this while a large proportion of the male farming population was drawn away from the fields to serve in the armed forces.

It must be admitted, however, that in comparison with the improved methods and implements introduced by the Agricultural Revolution in eighteenth-century Great Britain, much of Connecticut farming was still primitive and inefficient on the eve of the American Revolution. But, for perspective, we should recall that in Europe, the "old" agriculture had for centuries fed growing cities and produced the surpluses of wool, flax, flour, wheat, hemp, meat, and wine which had been staples in a flourishing international trade. In Europe, surplus crops had been produced with wooden plows edged with wrought iron, crude harrows, and iron hoes, while seed had been sown broadcast, and grain harvested with sickles and threshed with flails or by driving horses over grain on the bare barnyard. The small cattle, sheep, and hogs had grazed in common pastures far more frequently than not. Yet, they had produced the roast beef and pork pies of "Merrie England" and the wool for its growing woolen industry long before Jethro Tull and "Turnip" Lord Townsend introduced improvements in both soil fertility and mechanical equipment. For Connecticut on the eve of Lexington and Concord, therefore, we must examine its pre-modern agriculture for the light that this will cast upon its wartime performance.

By 1775, virtually all of Connecticut's land had been granted by the General Assembly, mostly to the proprietors of the self-governing towns, but also some directly to large landowners. By this time the unavailability of additional land for farms was causing an annual emigration of land-hungry farmers to New Hampshire, to the present state of Vermont, and to northern Pennsylvania. Four generations had elapsed since the settlement of Hartford, Windsor, Wethersfield, and Saybrook, and Connecticut was no longer a frontier commonwealth. During the long interim, the farmers of each town had cleared some of its forests to create fields and pastures, and had drained wet meadows in order to ensure ample hay crops and gain richer croplands. The frontier, in reality, had long been retreating in each town, as its inhabitants gathered pelts from the pests in the undivided forests, felled trees into planks, shingles, and staves, and grazed cattle and hogs in the woods during the summer to ease the pressure on inadequate pastures and maximize the hay crop to meet the need for winter forage. For the cleared lands, the town meetings had organized cooperative fencing of croplands, meadows, and pastures to protect them from the livestock, while assigning to each proprietor his share of each and of woodland from which he could draw fuel and wood for houses, barns, fences, and tools.

From the earliest days, the pelts and wood products had provided a surplus for farmers to exchange for salt, iron, and manufactured goods. An agricultural surplus also developed in the early settlements, when the annual increase of cattle from the towns and the Winthrops' large estates in eastern Connecticut were driven to Boston to be fattened and consumed as fresh meat or packed with salt in barrels for later consumption or export. Millers in water-powered grist mills in each town had taken their pay in a percentage of the wheat and rye brought to them for milling into flour. Local shopkeepers from the earliest days had brought the surplus cattle to Hartford's weekly market, as they did the millers' surplus wheat or flour, and exchanged both for imported goods. The local traders also bought any surplus from the salt meat that farm families barreled in the late autumn during the annual killing time when the herds of cattle and hogs, and the flocks of sheep were reduced to a size that could be winter fed. Wool from the spring sheep shearing and the autumn crop of flax were spun and woven into cloth for family use by the farmers' wives and daughters. Tanned hides from beeves and hogs provided leather for shoes and other uses, while each farmer's share of his water-ground flour provided bread. Barreled cider and pear brandy, pressed from the harvests of numerous orchards, were produced widely. Surplus cider, flaxseed from the flax crop, surplus hides, and salt meat and flour exceeding the family's needs were sold to the local shopkeeper in exchange for pewter, salt, superior English or India cloth, tea, and other luxury wares. All depended upon the merchants' ability to develop market outlets for the farmers' surpluses. And, as the number of farm families increased with the settlement of the colony between 1636 and 1775, the crops increased as more fields were cleared and tilled. As meadows and pastures expanded, the livestock swelled in numbers so rapidly as to create a chronic demand for hay and corn, far greater than the increasing supply.

This increasing agricultural surplus in Connecticut towns was the result, first of all, of the dynamics of land clearing and population growth as farmers sought farms for their sons, and as the legislature and town proprietors, at least until 1740, took in the stream of immigrants from already-overpopulated Massachusetts. The need for salt, and the desire for manufactured goods that made possible living above the frontier subsistence level, was another dynamic that induced farmers to produce surpluses. The ability of the average farmer to increase production, even after his farm of approximately 100 acres had been cleared, was limited. But larger landowners, from the days of Wait and Fitz-John Winthrop to those who received direct grants from the General Assembly, could employ farm laborers from the landless men and produce large surpluses of grain and livestock, while grazing the latter in separate pastures to avoid inbreeding down to a common scrub stock.

Production for market is, of course, commercial agriculture, and the first Connecticut farmers had been completely familiar with the methods of seventeenth-century English commercial agricultural production. Their first farm surpluses had been marketed overland in Boston via crude roads opened through the forests, although the small quantity and character of the produce had been determined by frontier conditions. But as these conditions passed, in town after town, the sale of increasing farm surpluses depended initially upon the Boston merchants' ability to open up markets for farm produce and wood products in the British West Indies, and for flour and salt provisions in Newfoundland and the Massachusetts shore towns which operated the ocean fishery. It was to these Boston merchants that the inland Connecticut merchants initially sent their colony's cattle, provisions, wheat, flour, and hides, while the rise of Boston as the region's metropolis provided a local market there for them as well.

During the eighteenth century, as Connecticut's frontier lands were settled by new towns, roads were opened up to navigable rivers or to Long Island Sound to facilitate the movement of farm surpluses to market. The merchants of Providence and Newport in Rhode Island, and of

Farms, such as this one in Reading, provided much of the food used by American forces during the Revolutionary War. From John W. Barber, *Connecticut Historical Collections.*

New York City on Manhattan Island in the royal province of New York, offered manufactured goods in competition with the Boston merchants and provided other markets to which Conecticut farm products could be taken by water or via new roads. To facilitate land transportation, Connecticut farmers bred oxen which, in yoked pairs, drew ploughs and harrows in the fields and pulled the sturdy, two-wheeled carts which facilitated farm operations and carried farm and wood products to points of transshipment by water. In 1770, a hundred such vehicles brought farm produce to New London each summer day.

Long before this, merchants had begun to operate at such other places in Connecticut as New Haven, Fairfield, Norwalk, Stamford, and Greenwich on the coast, and on the rivers at Norwich, Hartford, Wethersfield, Middletown, and Derby. These Connecticut traders sent vessels to the British and foreign West Indies with Connecticut produce, planks, and barrel staves, as well as coastwise to Boston and Newport, to Nantucket and Martha's Vineyard to supply the whalers, to Nova Scotia, to Marblehead to the cod fishery, to Newfoundland, and to New York City. Inland merchants at Woodbury, Litchfield, Danbury, and Waterbury, in western Connecticut, hauled flour and provisions to the Sound or to Derby, while Sharon merchants took Litchfield County flour overland to the Hudson River in New York. Drovers bought beef cattle and hogs in Yankee trading from farmers, and drove them to Boston, Providence, the Sound towns, and New York City. Increasingly, vessels took cattle, hogs, and sheep as deck cargoes to the West Indies. In the eighteenth century, they added horses to supply an insatiable plantation demand there for work horses and mules to operate the sugar mills, and for riding horses for the planters.

This market pressure produced significant developments in eighteenth-century Connecticut agriculture. The ability to sell ever-increasing quantities of provisions led to the development of autumn meat-packing as the colony's leading industry. It was organized at key locations such as Lebanon, near Norwich on the Thames River, by Jonathan Trumbull, or by drovers who were livestock specialists such as Colonel Henry Champion at Colchester, not far from East Haddam on the Connecticut River. Supplementing the killing and packing by all farm families, this industry provided an annual market for surplus beeves and hogs. Furthermore, since larger beef cattle and hogs produced a superior salt meat and brought higher prices, a premium was put on developing both. Oxen came to be bred to larger size for beef, as large as 1,600 pounds each by 1775, compared with those bred for draft purposes, which might average a mere 600 pounds. Enterprising farmers, especially large farm owners, discovered the profit accruable from feeding corn to lean cattle which, when fattened, could be sold to meat packers or to drovers for delivery to Boston, New York City, Providence, or the Sound ports. Such cattle feeders with large pastures in Litchfield County bought lean cattle from

New York and grass-fed them before finishing them off with corn. Other cattle feeders in Fairfield County bought local lean cattle before doing the same, as did enterprising farmers in Hartford County, where there was usually a bountiful corn crop. A similar activity was carried on at favorable locations in eastern Connecticut.

Such a livestock industry was far removed from the forest grazing of cattle and hogs during the colony's frontier phase. It was supported not only by a larger corn crop, but also by the introduction of oats, timothy hay, and clover, and by the exploitation of river and salt meadows for native hay. This supported the breeding of draft horses and Narragansett pacers, primarily with a view to the West Indies market, but also to meet the need for riding horses in Connecticut and the adjacent cities. Although such farmers occasionally employed horse-drawn wagons and used horse teams in cultivating their farms, the ox-cart and yoked oxen were far more typical in both land transportation and field cultivation.

Eighteenth-century Connecticut farmers found a market for butter and cheese made from surplus milk in the West Indies, Boston, Providence, Newport, and New York City, as well as the colony's own growing towns. A dairy operating at Stonington after 1770 sold its entire product of cheese and butter to Boston, and Massachusetts towns along the northeastern Connecticut boundary collected Connecticut cheese for transshipment to the New England metropolis. The small town of Lebanon regularly shipped butter and cheese to Boston, Nova Scotia, and Nantucket, and there is reason to believe that the products were of superior quality, especially in view of the old saying that "Connecticut looks to Lebanon for good cheeses and good governors." Thus, the production of dairy products was an important phase of the expansion of grazing at the expense of field crops that occurred in eastern Connecticut in the mid-eighteenth century, as farming there adjusted to the reality of thin soil and livestock opportunities.

In more favorable soil areas, such as the alluvial land of the Connecticut River Valley and along the Housatonic River north of Derby, the limestone belt in Litchfield County, and the flat lands of Fairfield County, crop production became important. One Litchfield County farmer, just before 1750, imported four new varieties of wheat from England in an attempt to increase wheat production. The well-defined wheat belt extended from Litchfield County east into Hartford County, south to the Middletown area, and north along the river until it joined a similar crop area in Berkshire and Hampshire Counties in western Massachusetts. Wheat in large surplus was also produced in Fairfield County, from which flour was sold to such New York City merchants as Peter Vandervoort who made something of a specialty of Connecticut grain and flour. This wheat and flour production in western Connecticut paralleled a large corn crop devoted to cattle and hog feeding for market. Before

1775, a small wheat surplus was also produced in inland eastern Connecticut.

Equally interesting was the development on the flat alluvial lands at Wethersfield on the Connecticut River of onion growing on a large commercial scale. Marketable as an important vegetable in the West Indies, northern cities, and the Connecticut towns, this crop increased until 100,000 ropes (or 2,000,000 pounds) were exported in 1774.

The figures of farm-produce exports, admittedly incomplete, illustrate how large was the agricultural surplus that Connecticut could place at the disposal of the war effort during 1775–1783. Certain it was that the farmers' ever-increasing surpluses enabled the merchants to exchange them for such West Indies products as rum, molasses, sugar, and coffee, with the Madeira and Canary Islands for wine, and in intercolonial trade for European and East Indian products. Immediately before 1774, Connecticut vessels exported annually some 15,000 head of livestock, 10,000 barrels of salt meat, 150,000 pounds of cheese, plus butter, poultry, wheat, corn, and flour, 30,000 bushels of flaxseed, and the 100,000 ropes of onions from Wethersfield. Highway traffic to Boston, Providence, and New York City carried out still more livestock, plus additional provisions, grain, and flour. Choice Connecticut salt pork was advertised in the Boston and New York newspapers. Lumber, staves, and potash produced on Connecticut farms found its way also to the West Indies or nearby New York City.

As early as 1750, the Reverend Jared Eliot, Congregational minister at Killingworth and the pioneer advocate of agricultural improvement in Connecticut, had reported how the marketing of the farmers' surpluses was improving their standard of living. This was evidenced by improved furniture, better food and clothing, finer houses, more elegant table silver and glass, and other luxuries. Likewise, the finer public buildings, the increase in the number of bridges over streams, the fatter cattle and better horses, and the steady rise in land values indicated substantial prosperity. Without doubt, it was this export trade which enabled the residents of the colony to live on a level of comfort which was then to be found in few parts of the world. By the outbreak of the Revolution, it was common for visitors from Europe and from other British North American colonies to marvel at the physical comfort enjoyed by all classes of Connecticut society.

Early in 1775, when Silas Deane and other leaders anticipated a clash between the colonial militia and General Thomas Gage's garrison in Boston, the tradition of colonial wars should have suggested to Connecticut statesmen the need to provide for supplying such Connecticut troops as might be called abruptly into the field. The practice during King George's War and the French and Indian War had been to contract with individual merchants to supply the militia employed in the imperial

Joseph Trumbull, Connecticut's first Commissary General during the American Revolutionary War. From a portrait by John Trumbull at the Connecticut Historical Society.

cause. Colonel Matthew Talcott of Middletown, an assemblyman in 1774–1775, had so supplied the Connecticut contingent in the 1745 expedition against Fort Louisbourg. Jonathan Trumbull, now governor, had been a contractor to supply the militia sent to Lake George and Lake Champlain against the Marquis de Montcalm during the French and Indian War. No advance arrangement was made in 1775, however, and the supply of such militia as might be called out to cope with an emergency was left to improvisation after the event.

When the "Lexington Alarm" informed Connecticut of the battles of Lexington and Concord, some 3,600 Sons of Liberty, volunteers, and militia rushed pell-mell to Cambridge to participate in an anticipated battle with General Gage. The special session of the General Assembly at Hartford on April 26 was presented with this makeshift force's need for food, tents, flints, lead, bullets, powder, and cooking and eating utensils. The leisurely procedures of negotiating with prospective contractors were out of the question. Instead, on April 26, the General Assembly established a commissariat to supply these troops. Joseph Trumbull, a bachelor ex-merchant practicing law at Norwich while serving on the Connecticut Committee of Correspondence, and son of the governor, was appointed Commissary General and sent to Cambridge to direct their supply. After considerable jockeying between the Council and the lower house of the General Assembly, nine commissaries were appointed "to supply all necessary Stores & provisions for the Troops now to be raised for the Defence of this Colony." An appeal from the Massachusetts Provincial Congress for 6,000 Connecticut militia to be part of an intercolonial army of 30,000 to oppose Gage in Boston had made such an arrangement desirable.

Each of the nine commissaries, most of whom had not been consulted in advance about their appointments, was a merchant skilled in bargaining for farm produce and other articles, accustomed to keeping the detailed records which the Committee of the Pay Table would require, and presumably capable of settling accounts for the expenditure of public funds to be supplied by Colony Treasurer John Lawrence. Each commissary was located in a town whose hinterland possessed an available surplus. Such were Amasa Keys at Pomfret, Hezekiah Bissell of Windham, Thomas Mumford at Groton on New London harbor, and Colonel Henry Champion at Colchester, all in eastern Connecticut. For western Connecticut, there were Captain Jeremiah Wadsworth of Hartford, Oliver Wolcott and Jedediah Strong of Litchfield, Thomas Howell of New Haven (quickly replaced by Jonathan Fitch), and Samuel Squire of Fairfield. Although each was to equip and supply the militia companies being called out in his area, no limitation was placed on the region from which he might draw supplies.

Three regiments were sent initially to Cambridge to replace the returning volunteers of the "Lexington Alarm." Also, the legislature called out two regiments to be stationed along the western shore to overawe New York Tories. A sixth regiment, under Colonel Samuel Holden Parsons, was stationed at New London for that town's protection. Then came the secret expedition against Fort Ticonderoga to secure its cannon for the army at Cambridge, and, perhaps even to the surprise of those who encouraged it, the mission was a success. A thousand militia were sent to Ticonderoga to hold it, pending action by the Continental Congress. The commissariat had to supply this force also, although at a considerable distance, with food, including beef and dairy cattle, sent from the colony. In all, some nine regiments called into active service had to be equipped and supplied regularly.

The General Assembly understood at once that this would be difficult, if not impossible, if exports of farm produce were to continue as usual. On the same day that it established the commissariat, the Assembly voted an immediate embargo on exportation by water out of the colony of wheat, rye, corn, pork, beef, live cattle, peas, beans, flour, and corn meal, except necessary stores for vessels bound to sea. To last initially only to May 20, when the regular session of the legislature could reconsider it, the embargo was immediately proclaimed by Governor Trumbull. When it was extended until August, the governor and the Council of Safety were empowered to embargo the export of any article during legislative recess. They were also empowered to grant permits for export by water of cattle and provisions. Thereafter, the embargo was extended regularly, and for four years it also applied to exports by land. Thus, embargo became a permanent feature of Connecticut's war policy. The embargo's initial purpose, obviously, was to reserve the colony's agricultural surplus for the supply of the regiments in the field. To this was quickly added supervised exports to the foreign West Indies by enterprising merchants such as Thomas Mumford and Nathaniel Shaw, Jr., of New London, for the purchase of powder. After the Continental Army was organized, Connecticut's embargo reserved its food surplus and scarce West India goods for the supply of the Continental Army, for the colony warships, and for the new Continental Navy that came into existence at the close of 1775.

The embargo made it possible for the commissaries to purchase beef cattle, hogs, sheep, provisions, flour, peas, beans, corn meal, and onions at 1774 prices or less, since there was no other large competing market. Ox teams with carts that had formerly hauled produce to salt or fresh-water wharves could be hired by each commissary to haul supplies to vessels waiting to carry them to Norwich, or to transport them from there or from the supplies' point of origin to Cambridge or other militia commands. With vessels scarce, and their captains frightened periodically by British naval incursions into the Sound, such commissaries as Jeremiah Wadsworth and Henry Champion took the precaution of having their supplies hauled by ox carts from Hartford, Glastonbury, and

East Haddam overland to Cambridge. Mumford secured supplies locally and from Fairfield County, sending them up the Thames River via Norwich, and then on ox carts to the camp on the Charles. Bissell and Keyes used ox carts exclusively for transportation from their inland towns. The commissaries took turns in escorting droves of livestock to camp.

From Cambridge, Commissary General Joseph Trumbull directed each commissary's procurement so far as it affected the supply of the Connecticut regiments there. But each commissary was obliged to employ his own initiative, subject to occasional directions from the governor, in equipping local companies, and in supplying them and such other companies as were stationed in his locality or marched through it on the way to Cambridge or Ticonderoga. Squire, for example, supplied the troops on the western shore and sent flour and provisions by water from Fairfield and Derby via New York City to Albany for transshipment to Ticonderoga. Jedediah Strong sent flour through Sharon and up the Hudson River to the same destination. Strong also sent Litchfield County peas via ox cart to Wadsworth at Hartford for forwarding to Cambridge. Wadsworth supplied companies en route as they passed through Hartford, and, on occasion, he opened his wife's kitchen to the company cooks, since no camp ground was provided in Hartford.

The need for tents to house the troops at Cambridge and elsewhere led the General Assembly and the governor to order the large-scale procurement of tow cloth, a coarse homemade linen fabric, and the manufacture of tents from it. Wadsworth systematically gathered all the tow cloth available from the towns in Hartford County and had the tents made by Peleg Sanford and other Middletown and Rocky Hill sailmakers. Joseph Trumbull, at his commissaries' suggestion, had the tent poles made in the Cambridge area.

In its May, 1775, session, the General Assembly adopted an official ration which gave specific direction to the commissaries' procurement. Quite generously, the daily ration was to include three quarters of a pound of salt or fresh pork or beef, a pound of bread or flour, and three pints of beer, plus unspecified amounts of milk, molasses, coffee, sugar, chocolate, vegetables, onions in season, vinegar, and weekly half a pint of rice or a pint of corn meal, six ounces of butter, three pints of peas or beans. Tobacco, candles, and soap were also to be provided. A gill of rum was to be issued daily to men on fatigue duty. The beer, incidentally, was a popular spruce beer made from a fermented mixture of molasses with essence of spruce derived from spruce needles and bows, a beverage whose manufacture Joseph Trumbull at Cambridge had to organize quickly while he arranged for the baking of bread and for a milk supply. Some of the Assembly's specifications were so vague as to require further definition by Brigadier Generals Joseph Spencer and Israel Putnam in special orders to Trumbull. The ration, however, was more generous than that provided by other New England commissaries to their respective militia, and it far surpassed the ration of the British regular army. The next January, Jedediah Huntington, colonel of a newly-raised Continental regiment of Connecticut troops, would learn from a British deserter that the ration of British troops in Boston consisted of "3 lb Pork p Man p week 5 oz Butter & 1 Gill Oil &c."

Each commissary had to range widely in his area in procuring the items included in the ration. There were difficulties as well in supplying tents, blankets, axes and digging tools, kettles of tin, iron, or brass, lead, spoons, bowls for serving food, and countless other items. Each commissary had to contract with tent makers, with millers, and with bakers. He had to employ assistants in purchasing, hire laborers to handle and load heavy articles on carts or vessels, pay suppliers and carters individually while negotiating with them for additional supplies and transportation, and keep a detailed record of his transactions. Intense zeal for the colonial cause during 1775, rather than the Assembly's stingy commission of 1½ per cent on purchases as compensation and to cover all costs, provided the chief motive for effective service, the more so since the regular mercantile commission on purchases for other merchants was 2 per cent. Included in the regular work of each Commissary was the inspection of provisions bought, and, as was frequently necessary, the opening of the barrels and repacking the salt meat with brine or salt to prevent spoiling.

At Cambridge, Joseph Trumbull rented quarters for the storage of flour, provisions, and other articles. Potatoes and onions, for example, were placed in the cellars of Harvard College. Trumbull established an office in which Elisha Avery, his assistant, supervised the commissaries who issued supplies to the troops, bought supplies brought in by private individuals, paid bills of the carters, and kept the Commissary General's books. In Massachusetts, Trumbull bought rice, rum, chocolate, molasses, coffee, milk, and bread. In addition to directing the work of the nine commissaries in Connecticut, he placed orders with two important Norwich merchants, Colonel Jabez Huntington and Christopher Leffingwell. Leffingwell, for example, via a succession of carters, sent seventeen bars of indispensable German steel for the armorers, plus salt pork, bread, and flour. Jabez Huntington forwarded ninety barrels of flour sent by Joseph Hallel of New York City on a contract with Congress. This indicated that Joseph Trumbull would not have to rely exclusively upon Connecticut flour, although Wadsworth, on June 15, assured him that the Hartford area alone possessed enough of it to supply all the Connecticut regiments at Cambridge. Wadsworth and the other commissaries, by advance contracting, blocked higher bidding for pork and flour by New Hampshire's agent. Meanwhile, the complete stoppage of western Connecticut pork shipments to New York by the embargo had precipitated vain protests against it from New York merchants and General Philip Schuyler.

Insight into the effect of the embargo on the prices for food that

Connecticut commissaries had to pay is provided by John Olcott's bill of August 5, 1775, to Jeremiah Wadsworth. This reveals that a year earlier, on April 26, 1774, Wadsworth had paid 60s. per barrel for salt pork shipped on his vessel to the West Indies, but that in buying twenty barrels of pork for the public between May 21 and August 3, 1775, in three separate purchases, he paid Olcott only 57s.

Wadsworth and the four commissaries who operated east of the Connecticut River bore the chief responsibility for supplying Joseph Trumbull and the Connecticut regiments at Cambridge. Since Champion was a noted beef specialist, Wadsworth and the other commissaries agreed that he should concentrate on beef-cattle procurement. This arrangement led to dispatching superior beeves to Cambridge. Joseph Trumbull approved. Wadsworth recommended that fresh meat be supplied four days a week to the Connecticut troops so as to save the high cost of carting so much provisions to Cambridge at £10 per cart carrying 2,500 pounds a trip. In this recommendation, Generals Spencer and Putnam and their colonels concurred.

On Wadsworth's recommendation, also, Trumbull ordered the establishment of flour magazines at Pomfret, on the road to Cambridge, and others at Medfield and Southborough, Massachusetts. Wadsworth held the price of flour at Hartford at 13s. per hundredweight, and he resisted attempts of the Massachusetts Committee of Supplies to buy flour there lest this raise the price. Although merchant William Hubbard of Norwich urged him in his commissary work "to be as favourable to yourself as the nature of your *call* will admit of," Wadsworth refused to pay the higher prices which would have netted him larger commissions. Thus, patriotism rather than sheer acquisitiveness controlled his conduct of public business. So motivated, Wadsworth sent by cart from Glastonbury alone 160 barrels of flour to Medfield and Southborough.

When the commissaries alternated trips to Cambridge with their livestock droves, Trumbull informed them of specific needs, coordinated their activities, and gave verbal orders, which he supplemented with letters to each. On quick trips to eastern Connecticut, Trumbull conferred with Keyes, Wadsworth, and the Norwich merchants. By such means, he achieved a successful coordination of the supply of the Connecticut regiments at Cambridge. He provided for them much better than did either the Massachusetts Committee of Supplies or the New Hampshire commissaries for their provincial troops.

Meanwhile, under orders from Treasurer Lawrence, Wadsworth bought 2,360 pounds of lead and bullets in Wethersfield, Rocky Hill, and Middletown to replace that which had been expended in the Battle of Bunker Hill. In a single day at Hartford, he filled Joseph Trumbull's order for 600 barrels of salt pork (500 for Massachusetts troops, 100 for the New Hampshire militia) in return for which Massachusetts would supply the Connecticut regiments with fish. While at Cambridge, when

General George Washington assumed command of the newly-created Continental Army, Wadsworth's agent, Justus Riley, contracted with Captain Ebenezer Gray at Derby for 970 barrels of salt pork to be delivered at Hartford for 54s. a barrel, six shillings below the 1774 price. Despite a prolonged drought, Wadsworth had so many mills under contract that his supply of flour was assured. Thus, whatever might be the effect of the new organization of the army before Boston upon the Connecticut commissaries, the Connecticut regiments there would be supplied. Then it rained. Wadsworth promised Trumbull flour "for the whole army." As the crop ripened, he began to include onions in his shipments. On July 10th, Joseph Trumbull wrote that he expected "all our Regt of Commissaries will soon be disbanded, & myself at the head of them."

Although a Continental Commissary Department was soon created to supply the new army, the Connecticut commissaries continued to draw funds from Treasurer Lawrence and to send supplies to Joseph Trumbull until October, 1775. In November, the Pay Table reported to the General Assembly on the money that had been paid to them. Joseph Trumbull had received £6,791.19.8. (The Connecticut pound was then worth $3.33.) Among the commissaries, Jeremiah Wadsworth had far exceeded the others with £13,450; Mumford was next with £9,130; Squire had received £6,500; Champion £6,400; and Fitch £6,500. The grand total was £56,951.8.2.

That nine regiments could have been supplied for five months with so modest a sum can be explained only by the low level of prices that the commissaries paid. Prices paid for tents, lead, shovels, pickaxes, spades, iron and brass kettles, paper and quills, wooden bowls, and Suffield bowls were moderate indeed, as were the wages paid to personnel.

Jeremiah Wadsworth's account with the Colony of Connecticut for May 6–August 2, 1775, lists the prices paid by him for various articles, and these were probably typical of commissary procurements for that period. For six yokes of oxen, Wadsworth paid from £15 to £20 per yoke, plus four shillings for yoke, staple, and ring, and £5.6.0. for each cart. He paid 6s.6d. per ax, 1s.4d. to 1s.7½d. per yard of tow cloth, 4s. for tin kettles, 3s. for sacking bags for peas and beans, 1s.6d. per barrel, 3s.6d. to 9s. per cask. For grain, he paid 2s.4d. per bushel for ears of corn, 2s.6d. to 2s.8d. per bushel for rye, 1s.6d. to 3s.9d. per bushel of oats. He paid 4s. to 4s.6d. per bushel of beans, 6s. for a bushel of peas, 2s.6d. per bushel of corn meal, for bread 18s. to 20s. per hundredweight, and for butter 8d. a pound. He bought salt pork at from 54s. to 60s. per barrel, rum for 3s.3d. per gallon, flour for 13s. (usually) to 20s. (rarely) a cwt, claret at 30s. a dozen (for Washington's mess), and £11 for a quarter cask of Madeira wine (for Joseph Trumbull's mess). Dr. Smith's bill for "Medicin &c" was £63.13.9. Loaf sugar was 14d. a pound, and coffee 10d.

Some conception of the equipment that each commissary had to provide for the regiment raised in his district can be gathered from the resolution adopted by the General Assembly's special session on July 1, 1775. This ordered that each of the two additional regiments to be raised be supplied with 48 marquee tents for officers, 233 tents for privates, 281 ten-quart tin or iron pots, 14 eight to twelve-quart brass kettles, 600 wooden bowls, 3 frying pans per company, 1,400 quart runlets, 20 drums, 40 fifes, a medicine chest worth £30, fourteen books in quarto, half a ream of writing paper, three reams of cartridge paper, and one cart or wagon per company. All this had to be supplied from within the colony.

In late July at Philadelphia, Silas Deane anticipated General Washington's recommendation and persuaded Congress to unanimously appoint Joseph Trumbull Commissary General of the Continental Army with the rank and salary of colonel. This satisfied Washington's desire for a Continental Commissary to provide food, salt, soap, and candles for the army, paralleling a Quartermaster Department to provide transportation, forage, repair of arms, etc. By implication only, Congress permitted Trumbull to employ needed subordinates, but it established no method of compensation other than belatedly to vote salaries to his headquarters office staff. By contrast, Congress paid Quartermaster General Colonel Thomas Mifflin on commission and permitted him to compensate his subordinates with a 2 per cent commission on their expenditures.

Confident that he could eventually persuade Congress to allow him to compensate his purchasing commissaries by commission also (which it never officially did), Trumbull developed a dual organization. Half of it procured supplies and sent them to his magazines. The other half administered the magazines and delivered supplies to the several commands, where other commissaries issued them directly to the troops. For the purchasing section of the Commissary, Trumbull took over from the New England provincial commissaries the most energetic and reliable purchasers and appointed others. In addition, Trumbull himself contracted directly with leading merchants for large quantities of supplies. In Connecticut, for example, he retained Wadsworth, Champion, Keyes, Mumford, Fitch, and Squire, and added Captain Samuel McClellan of Woodstock and Daniel Gray of Stamford to his corps of purchasers. Champion and Wadsworth promptly bought together over 2,000 barrels of pork in western Connecticut. Simultaneously, Trumbull contracted for supplies with Leffingwell and Jabez Huntington of Norwich and with Shaw at New London.

During the transitional months of July and August, the Connecticut commissaries continued to send supplies to the Connecticut regiments at Cambridge and elsewhere, and Wadsworth, under orders, supplied the colony-armed brig *Minerva*. In mid-September, the governor and Council of Safety stopped Treasurer Lawrence's advances of funds to the colony's commissaries. As Commissary General of the Continental Army,

Although this ship, the *General Putnam*, was a privateer, it is similar to those used by Connecticut as supply vessels. From Louis F. Middlebrook, *Maritime Connecticut During the American Revolution, 1775–1783*, Volume II.

Joseph Trumbull had to rely thenceforth entirely upon Continental currency. At first he drew upon Washington's military chest, whose funds arrived belatedly and in insufficient quantity. As a result, Trumbull's purchasers in Connecticut were left periodically without funds to pay for supplies on delivery, or to compensate carters on their return from hauling supplies to the magazines. Dunned incessantly by suppliers and carters, such a purchaser as Wadsworth was humiliated by his inability to pay his bills. He confided to his diary, as a former ship captain, that he must "avoid this rock again." Finally, when Trumbull was seriously ill from dysentery at Lebanon, Wadsworth went to Cambridge for him and secured $120,000 from Washington and this relieved the immediate financial stringency. But Congress's failure to remit funds promptly was to cause another crisis in February, 1776.

Meanwhile, during August and September, 1775, Trumbull had urged Wadsworth and the other purchasers to send to the magazines large quantities of flour and salt pork so that he could build a reserve of three-months' supply against contingencies. Each colony, Trumbull told Wadsworth, should provide its staple, and Connecticut's staple was salt pork. Upon Massachusetts, obviously, he relied for fish. Wadsworth sent 178 barrels of pork from Hartford to the magazines between July 1 to September 14. He also sent 1,000 barrels more from other Connecticut River towns. In four months, Wadsworth sent 941 bushels of peas. Wadsworth and Champion ordered that the western Connecticut pork that they had contracted for be sent by water to Norwich. But their ship captains, frightened by British naval activity, landed it at East Haddam on the river. From there it was carted the long distance to Medfield and Southborough.

While procuring flour in Hartford County, Wadsworth was handicapped by a combination of the suppliers, who sought to advance the price, and by the intervention of the Massachusetts Committee of Supplies, which contracted with Asbell Steel and James Shepard, Hartford merchants, for 500 barrels of flour. Wadsworth resisted the suppliers' combination. He blocked Steel and Shepard's operations by contracting with the mills they relied upon, and he persuaded Trumbull to order the Massachusetts Committee of Supplies to desist from further procurement in Connecticut. Aside from a short-lived price rise precipitated by Steel and Shepard's activity, Wadsworth held the flour price in Hartford county to 13s. a hundredweight. From Hartford Wadsworth sent 259 barrels before August 3, and 220 barrels in the next two days. Between May, 1775, and June, 1776, he sent 6,775 barrels to Trumbull's magazines, most of it bought at 13s. from a large number of suppliers. At Washington's request via Governor Trumbull, Wadsworth also had hundreds of tow cloth hunting shirts made for the Connecticut and Rhode Island regiments.

Simultaneously, McClellan, Keyes, Mumford, Leffingwell, and Jabez Huntington sent to Joseph Trumbull all available pork, butter, peas, and flour from eastern Connecticut. By August 3, McClellan had sent 819 barrels of flour, and Leffingwell had provided 276 barrels. Mumford, Leffingwell, and Huntington procured much pork, peas, and flour from Fairfield County. Mumford even lost, albeit temporarily, his fear of the British fleet, and shipped beans, butter, flour, peas, and pork to Providence for the shorter overland haul to Medfield. Squires and Gray sent large quantities of flour and pork, drawing upon Derby and Woodbury for both. Then Squire's and Strong's supply of Ticonderoga was stopped when Congress appointed an independent Deputy Commissary General, Walter Livingston, for the Northern Department. Livingston contracted for pork with one Van Rensalaer, who promptly asked Governor Trumbull for permission to ship 450 barrels from Connecticut to Albany. Recognizing the Northern Army's need, the governor issued the permit and directed Wadsworth to release to Van Rensalaer this amount from his purchases and expedite the shipment. Finding that he had to rely upon western Connecticut for salt pork, Livingston contracted with Abraham Livingston of New York City for a supply.

As Commissary General, Joseph Trumbull also contracted directly with merchants outside of Connecticut for large quantities of supplies. He secured thereby raisins, low-priced wines, tamarinds (for medicine), New England rum, West India goods from Newburyport, 2,000 barrels of flour from Wilbraham, and rum and molasses from Dartmouth, all in Massachusetts, as well as rum, wine, and various other items from Providence. While Trumbull supplied 300 barrels of Connecticut pork to Colonel Benedict Arnold's secret expedition against Quebec, he was confident that, since the Commissary was the only large buyer, and Connecticut's embargo was enforced, he could control the flour market.

On August 31, Trumbull wrote to Wadsworth, "look sharp don't let it be said Connecticut can't support 30,000 men themselves maugre all the Vile arts of New York, who intend to starve us if they can." Trumbull was, of course, alluding to New Yorkers' large export of flour to Antigua when the army's supply was short, and also to the combination of New York flour merchants to maintain the price of 20s. Trumbull learned of this high price from Peter Vandervoort and Isaac Sears, with whom he contracted for two successive lots of 10,000 barrels of flour, plus butter, corn, and peas in order to build up his magazines. This followed Joseph Hallet's shipment of 5,000 barrels of flour from New York on his contract with Congress. Vandervoort and Sears procured their peas in the Albany area, but they bought much of their flour, butter, and corn in Fairfield and Litchfield Counties, Connecticut, while charging the New York flour price, which they eventually lowered to 18s. The high New York flour price led Fairfield and Litchfield County farmers to cart much of their wheat into that state, since the embargo at that time applied only to water shipments.

Joseph Trumbull sent his brother, Jonathan, Jr., to Philadelphia in an attempt to contract for flour there, but Jonathan was blocked in Congress by the New York delegation, which protested effectively against the allegedly higher cost of Pennsylvania flour and the great risk of shipping it by water. Vandervoort and Sears shipped theirs through Long Island Sound to Leffingwell and Huntington at Norwich. Since Joseph Trumbull was Commissary General for the Continental Army, there was no objection to his contracting with sources of supply outside of Connecticut, but the extortion practiced by the New York flour merchants was known there and precipitated heated but vain protests against Wadsworth's low price for Connecticut flour.

Joseph Trumbull relied upon Connecticut first of all for salt pork, and second for a large proportion of his supply of fresh beef. Experiencing irregular deliveries of beef cattle, with alternate periods of dearth and oversupply, he put Champion in charge of providing beeves for Washington's army. He contracted exclusively with Champion, with the understanding that he receive beeves also from Massachusetts, New Hampshire, and Rhode Island suppliers, and include cattle removed from exposed coastal regions on Washington's order.

As the late autumn killing time approached, and as Connecticut hog owners inquired for the price that Trumbull would pay for pork on the hoof or salted down in barrels, Wadsworth urged him to have the provisions required for Washington's army in 1776 packed near camp where salt could be supplied readily by Massachusetts merchants. After securing authorization from Congress, Trumbull contracted with Champion, Keyes, and William Deming (of Colchester) to pack a large quantity of pork and then of beef at Medfield and Roxbury. He fixed prices per pound for small and large hogs at such figures as would attract large droves of them from eastern, central, and even western Connecticut. Trumbull also agreed to buy barreled salt pork at a competitive price if delivered to the magazine. Champion, Keyes, and Deming packed 3,600 barrels of pork at Medford and Roxbury, and then they processed a large quantity of beef from Connecticut droves. Paralleling their operations was that of Oliver Phelps of Granville, Massachusetts, who packed 2,000 barrels of pork under a similar contract with Trumbull. Phelps drove hogs from western, central, and eastern Massachusetts to his packing station at Jamaica Plain. This dual operation saved the heavy cost of land transportation that would have been required if the hogs and beeves had been packed in the towns where they had been raised. Trumbull now possessed large magazines of provisions close to Washington's army.

Meanwhile, Trumbull imported by vessel from Maine spruce needles and bows for brewing spruce beer. He also had bread baked at Newburyport. To thwart Massachusetts oats speculators, Quartermaster General Mifflin bought 2,000 bushels of that grain from Wadsworth at Hartford. As ordered by Trumbull, Wadsworth also bought all available beans and peas in western Connecticut for the army's winter supply. Trumbull received his soap from a Cambridge contractor. Norwich and Stonington cheese in quantity was made available to him, while other Connecticut cheese, plus butter, came through the Massachusetts border town of Westborough.

Before the Vandervoort and Sears flour shipments began to arrive at Norwich in September, 1775, Joseph Trumbull had relied briefly upon Wadsworth for his supply. Then, in January, 1776, Washington persuaded Governor Trumbull and the Connecticut Council of Safety to send 2,000 militia to New York City to be commanded initially by General Charles Lee. Confident that he would soon expel General William Howe's army from Boston, after which his own army would move to New York City, Washington ordered Joseph Trumbull to draw no more flour from that source, and to conserve the supply there for the army's future use. Joseph Trumbull promptly informed Wadsworth on January 11th and gave him and Connecticut the sole supply of flour for the army at Cambridge, remarking that this was only just, since Vandervoort and Sears had drawn so much of their contract quantity from that colony.

Trumbull did not remark upon the obvious saving that the Commissary would make from buying Wadsworth's flour at 13s. In contrast with Wadsworth and Champion's price of 54s. for western Connecticut pork, Vandervoort had paid 80s. and charged Trumbull accordingly. It was obvious that Trumbull's Connecticut purchasers supplied him during 1775–1776 with a much greater regard for thrift. Squire had informed him from Fairfield in late October that after Vandervoort and Sears had profited largely from shipping to him thousands of barrels of west-Connecticut flour, there was still a great quantity of old wheat ready to be milled, which, together with butter and beef cattle, if wanted, he could send direct. Jonathan Fitch also had sent much pork and flour from New Haven to Mumford for forwarding. All the western purchasers, such as Squire, who sent much flour and pork to Mumford and Leffingwell, and Gray, who sent much flour to Trumbull from Stamford, had to pay higher prices because of the activity of Vandervoort and Sears and the influence of the New York market. Probably western Connecticut contributed more extensively to the supply of the Continental Army at Cambridge before March 1776 via Trumbull's purchasers than it did via Vandervoort and Sears' earlier operation. Only cider, the universal beverage in Connecticut, was omitted from the food and drink sent. For some unexplained reason, the General Assembly had omitted cider from the Connecticut ration, and the Connecticut ration had now become the basis of the ration of the Continental Army.

The hides from daily slaughtering at the Cambridge and Roxbury camps had been saved and shipped back to Connecticut tanners to be made into leather and then into shoes and other leather goods, a portion of which went to the army. The ingenious Wadsworth, who was Joseph

Trumbull's chief adviser, foreseeing a great winter need for blankets, had bought Long Island wool and employed scores of Connecticut women to produce them by hundreds before Washington appealed to Governor Trumbull in early January for blankets for his newly-recruited regiments. Then, Wadsworth led in persuading the towns to equip each new recruit for Connecticut Line regiments with a blanket before he left home. Refusing 20 per cent profit on his operation from private traders, he also collected and sent to Cambridge coarse woolens for coats for the shivering troops. Wadsworth kept Washington's and Joseph Trumbull's messes supplied with Madeira, while Clark and Nightingale of Providence sent Teneriffe and other wines.

Wadsworth bitterly resented popular criticism in Connecticut of the commissaries, particularly the attacks by those who conspired to raise prices. He was gratified, therefore, when his friend and collaborator, Henry Champion, was completely vindicated in a public hearing before the General Assembly at New Haven in October, 1775, from charges that he had contracted at exorbitant prices to enrich himself, his relatives, and his friends.

When Washington seized Dorchester Heights and forced Howe's evacuation from Boston in early March, 1776, he instructed Joseph Trumbull to prepare for the army's removal to New York City. Envisaging a route via Hartford and New Haven, Trumbull ordered Wadsworth to make the necessary preparations. Buying pork himself for the march between Hartford and New Haven, Wadsworth employed James Church of Farmington to direct the baking of bread at Hartford, asked Champion to supply beef, and sent Peter Colt, Fitch's New Haven partner, to contract for flour and pork at stopping points for the army's supply along the Western Shore. Then Washington's brigades marched instead to Norwich and New London. Trumbull's purchasers and merchant friends improvised their supply in eastern Connecticut and chartered vessels to transport them to New York City. At Lebanon, Trumbull told Wadsworth that he confronted a new era in supplying the Continental Army. It was necessary to stop the stream of supplies moving to Cambridge and redirect it to Manhattan Island.

This was accomplished quickly with a minimum of confusion. Sufficient pork was procured in central and western Connecticut to meet the army's needs at Trumbull's price of $10 to $10.50 a barrel. New York flour stored in New London and Norwich was shipped back to Manhattan on the transports carrying the troops. In the city, Joseph Trumbull was given the cellars of the hospital to use as a storage magazine. His thrifty price of pork, however, was too low in Connecticut to enable Major Abel and Thaddeus Burr to procure the 4,000 barrels of pork contracted with Abram Livingston for the Northern Army. But at Hartford the movement of Washington's army to New York brought down the price of flour and enabled Wadsworth to buy a large supply which he sent with pork on vessels to that city. After he rushed a drove of cattle there to meet an emergency, Champion regularized the beef supply again as the main supplier. Daniel Gray at Stamford now became one of Trumbull's leading purchasers in Connecticut, reaching up to Woodbury and east to Derby for pork and flour. Fitch and Colt drew heavily upon the resources of the New Haven area. Jabez Huntington sent salt from Norwich. Molasses and West India rum were sent by Mumford and Shaw. Trumbull's dependence upon Connecticut increased as he assumed responsibility for supplying pork to Schuyler's command at Albany and to the sickly Army of Canada after its retreat to Ticonderoga. Trumbull's responsibility for the general supply of both became direct when Congress permitted him to replace Walter Livingston as northern deputy with Elisha Avery, a Connecticut man. Connecticut's new embargo on West India goods also worked to Trumbull's advantage in ensuring the army a certain supply of molasses, rum, and coffee.

Trumbull drew upon New York for large quantities of flour after he persuaded its Convention to stop the export of that commodity. A large flour reserve was accumulated both at New York City and at Albany, and this was supplemented with additional flour bought in Philadelphia. As New Jersey and Pennsylvania militia gathered at Perth Amboy and Newark, Trumbull organized their supply from New Jersey resources by employing Robert Ogden of Elizabeth Town and Colonel Azariah Dunham of New Brunswick for the purpose. At Boston, he placed Charles Miller in charge of the magazines left behind by Washington, with Miller taking responsibility for supplying the garrison protecting that port. At Granville in west Massachusetts, Oliver Phelps contracted to supply Avery's Northern Department with beef cattle, salt beef, etc. Thus, Trumbull's organization and procurement became interregional in character, although his exclusive control of supplying the Continental armies was challenged when the New York Convention gave Abram Livingston a contract to supply Fort Constitution in the Highlands on the Hudson River. Within Connecticut, Trumbull's purchasers temporarily supplied three regiments of Connecticut militia stationed on the shore and three companies protecting the cannon foundry at Salisbury. For all these supply operations, Trumbull thriftily fixed low prices for procurement, i.e., below 13s. for flour, no higher than $11 for pork, thus capitalizing upon the Connecticut embargo while accumulating large supplies.

Washington had praised Trumbull's performance in the Commissary to Congress in August, 1775. He was equally satisfied with him when the New York City campaign began in July, 1776.

After the defeat and capture of Major General John Sullivan in the Battle of Long Island, Trumbull foresaw Washington's eventual retreat from Manhattan to the mainland. Quickly he ordered Wadsworth, now his deputy for all the territory east of the Hudson River, to establish a large magazine at Saw Pits near Rye on Long Island Sound and another at Kings Bridge on the Harlem River. Wadsworth did so, drawing heavily on shipments of supplies sent by vessel from Norwich, New London, Hartford, Middletown, and New Haven to Stamford. From there, employing ox teams bought at Colchester, he transported these supplies to Saw Pits and a second depot at Mamaroneck, New York. From these points, some supplies were transferred to Kings Bridge. These magazines became indispensable when Washington's army moved to White Plains after the Battle of Harlem Heights. The eight Connecticut militia regiments which were sent as a reinforcement also drew from them. Ogden, Dunham, Carpenter Wharton, and William Lowry supplied the militia holding eastern New Jersey.

Washington's sudden evacuation of New York City had obliged him to abandon the great reserve of flour that Trumbull had accumulated there. Washington left a smaller quantity behind when he retreated to Croton River after Howe's victory in the Battle of White Plains. As a result, the Continental Army faced a serious bread shortage. Wadsworth sent Colt up the Hudson Valley to procure an emergency supply. He persuaded Connecticut's General Assembly to authorize the Commissary to seize wheat and flour from farmers and merchants who withheld them in the hope of higher prices, while Daniel Gray shipped flour and provisions by wagon on a roundabout road to the army. Trumbull went to Norwich, where he had a flour reserve, and expedited shipments to Stamford, from which point they were forwarded by Gray. Thus, the flour crisis was surmounted.

Meanwhile, Howe's sudden capture of Forts Lee and Washington on the Hudson had divided Washington's army and complicated its supply. While a portion of this force remained at Fort Constitution, Peekskill, and Fishkill on the Hudson River, Washington was obliged to retreat rapidly with the remainder of his army across New Jersey. Trumbull was torn between the need to supply Washington's shrinking, rapidly-moving force, and the need to go to New England to organize large scale packing of provisions for the next campaign, and where, in intervals of leisure, he could prepare his books for the Board of Accounts. After sending his accounts on to Hartford, Trumbull, at Morristown, New Jersey, appointed Carpenter Wharton of Philadelphia as deputy to support Washington's army. He then persuaded Washington to allow him to go to Hartford to attend to departmental business. Wharton, however, delegated his responsibility to William Lowry of West New Jersey, and Lowry, unfortunately, neglected Washington's command. After Washington's troops had won victories at both Trenton and Princeton, at the latter without provisions, Lowry appeared and resigned. Furious, Washington appointed Mathew Irwin, Trumbull's Philadelphia flour buyer, deputy for New Jersey and Pennsylvania to supply the army, and demanded that Trumbull come to winter headquarters at Morristown.

Trumbull waited until late April to obey that order, having found time, upon his return from New Jersey, to marry Amelia, the daughter of Colonel Eliphalet Dyer, his father's old ally in Connecticut politics, and it was at Windham that Joseph Trumbull settled down with his bride. Not all of his time was devoted to Amelia, however, for with Wadsworth's aid, he directed the packing of an unprecedented quantity of salt pork and salt beef. He sledded large amounts of them over the heavy snow to Albany to stock the Northern Department's magazine. Trumbull also sent Wadsworth as his personal deputy to inspect departmental magazines and stores of the Hudson River command, and then to Morristown to see Irwin and consult with Washington. After consulting also with Robert Morris at Philadelphia, Wadsworth restricted Wharton to meat packing in Pennsylvania and restored the Commissary there and in New Jersey to functioning. Wharton, however, antagonized Congress by paying excessive prices for hogs and beeves. Washington was angered when Trumbull failed to stock the Hudson River magazines so as to enable Major General Alexander McDougall to maneuver. Trumbull returned to headquarters in April under a dual cloud. There he was confronted by Roger Sherman, a member of a congressional committee, with a certain Baltimore merchant's alternative proposals that he be either permitted to supply the armed forces by contract or that the Commissary be divided into purchasing and issuing departments.

Trumbull removed Wharton and his subordinates from the Commissary, but their delay in handing over magazines straitened the army's supply at Morristown. Trumbull was obliged to spend weeks in Philadelphia consulting with the congressional committee. There, he defeated the proposal to supply the armed forces by contract, but he was unable to block the committee's determination to divide his department and create a Commissary of Purchases and a Commissary of Issues. Sherman, the dominant figure, rejected the Baltimore merchant's and Trumbull's insistence that the deputies and purchasing commissaries in the former be paid by commission. Instead, the committee persuaded Congress to pay them niggardly salaries, provide for inadequate clerical help, and make the deputies independent of the Commissary General of Purchases, who was thus unable to coordinate their activities or direct their procurement. Sherman and his followers in Congress believed that each deputy would be able to supply the armed forces in his department from its resources. Quixotically, Sherman did not appreciate the central importance of Connecticut in the coordinated interstate system of supply that Trumbull was operating. Although he was appointed Commissary General of Purchases, Trumbull resigned when his demand for adequate authority and pay by commission was rejected. Wadsworth, Avery, Champion, and numerous purchasing and issuing commissaries resigned also. Joseph Trumbull died on July 23, 1778, and his family, probably not without reason, insisted that his early end was brought on by overwork.

Meanwhile, on June 11, 1777, Congress spelled out the dual organization of the commissary in 7,000 words of impossible regulations, the most bizarre of which was that the initials of cattle suppliers be carved on the horns of the cattle they delivered. The Commissary of Issues was to perform the annual meat packing, whereas the purchasing commissaries had always directed it in the past. The inexperienced Colonel William Buchanan of Maryland was appointed Commissary General of Purchases, and the equally inexperienced Colonel Charles Stewart was given the post of Commissary General of Issues. Delays of months ensued before the two departments were organized, the Purchases under deputies named by Congress, while ill-supplied Washington opposed Howe's campaign against Philadelphia.

Although Jeremiah Wadsworth was now out of office with no successor as deputy in Purchases in control of the magazines in his former Eastern Department, Wadsworth supplied provisions for Major General Horatio Gates's successful opposition to General Sir John Burgoyne and for Major General Israel Putnam's defense of the Hudson River. After the victory at Saratoga, Wadsworth handed over Purchases to Peter Colt as eastern deputy and the magazines to Samuel Gray, Eastern Deputy of Issues, and planned to go to sea in command of a new privateer.

Then the Commissary of Purchases, William Buchanan, refused to pack the provisions necessary for the next campaign. Unable to inspire confidence in his capacity, Buchanan failed to wangle funds from the Board of Treasury. Left without money, deeply in debt, Colt was unable to support adequately the commands at Boston and Providence and Putnam's command in winter quarters at Redding, Connecticut. The latter troops experienced the same semi-starvation as did Washington's reduced command at Valley Forge. For its supply, Colonel Ephraim Blaine, deputy of the Middle Department, lacked money also and was unable to collect sufficient supplies from the adjacent area as Congress demanded.

Upon receipt of a desperate appeal from Washington for beef cattle, Governor Trumbull and his Council of Safety invoked authority granted them by Congress and appointed Henry Champion Deputy Commissary General of Purchases for the Eastern Department for the procurement of beef cattle. After he received $200,000 that had been sent by Congress, Champion scoured the country for live beef, bought successive droves of Connecticut beeves, and, with his sons, escorted them overland to Valley Forge just in time to prevent complete starvation there. So desperate was the food situation in Washington's winter camp that the first herd of over a score of cattle was devoured within five days by the ravenous soldiers. Previous to this, under Governor Trumbull's orders, Champion had persuaded the Connecticut River Valley towns to pack provisions. Now he persuaded the cattle feeders to resume operations since he could provide them with a market.

Obviously, the very survival of the Continental armed forces in 1778 depended upon the restoration of effective military staff departments that would revive a well-organized, coordinated system of interstate supply and be directed by competent, experienced men. Washington recognized this. He informed the alarmed committee that Congress sent to Valley Forge that the inactive Quartermaster Department and the Commissary of Purchases must be headed by such men, who *themselves* must draft the regulations under which they could operate effectively. When Wadsworth refused appointment as Quartermaster General, Washington persuaded Congress to name Major General Nathanael Greene to that post and to accept his new regulations. Then Washington demanded that Congress appoint Wadsworth, Trumbull's brilliant former deputy, Commissary General of Purchases. The reluctant Wadsworth was told by Governor Trumbull and the Council of Safety that he must accept Congress's call. But he went to York, Pennsylvania, where Congress was sitting, to confer with its committee. Wadsworth determined not to accept appointment unless he could establish a totally new system for the Commissary of Purchases into which he intended to interweave Trumbull's rejected demands with regulations based upon his own broad experience. Thus, whereas Trumbull had improvised the organization of the old Commissary as he extended it to include the Middle States in addition to New England where it had originated, Wadsworth succeeded in persuading Congress to allow him to create a national organization in the Commissary of Purchases from which only South Carolina and Georgia were excluded.

In this reorganized Commissary of Purchases, with its five departments (Eastern, Northern, Middle, Southern, and Western), Connecticut, together with Massachusetts, Rhode Island, and Dutchess and Westchester Counties of New York, belonged to the small Eastern Department under deputies Peter Colt and Henry Champion. During the summer of 1777 in the Middletown area of Hartford county, once Connecticut's leader in wheat production, the ravages of the Hessian fly had so discouraged farmers that they had substituted rye largely for wheat in their planting. This reduced Connecticut's ability to produce a surplus of flour for the armed forces.

Furthermore, the General Assembly's adoption of a stringent but ill-conceived price-fixing act in February, 1778, had suddenly paralyzed Colt's procurement and Champion's beef-cattle buying, and stopped the operations of cattle feeders who had loyally supported his supply of the armies previously under Joseph Trumbull. Since Congress had sponsored the northern interstate New Haven price-fixing convention in January, where Roger Sherman had led in recommending this policy to the states, both congressional pride and Connecticut policy were roadblocks in the way of effective operation of the reorganized Commissary of Purchases under Jeremiah Wadsworth.

After he had deftly won from Congress complete authority over his deputies and their assistant purchasing commissaries, with pay by commission for both himself and his subordinates, Wadsworth was promised adequate financial support. By demonstrating that supply of the armed forces would otherwise be impossible, he also won a pledge that Congress would recommend suspension of the price-fixing acts of Connecticut, New Jersey, and other states. After appraising individually the capabilities of the deputies that he inherited from Buchanan's ineffective organization, Wadsworth retained them but subjected them to his personal supervision and procurement policy. Colt and Champion he knew personally, and he regarded them "as sure as death." With their approval, after he returned temporarily to Hartford, he waged a successful campaign for suspension of the Connecticut price-fixing act.

Meanwhile, as he supplied his deputies with funds, he was able to restore effective supply of the armed forces within six weeks, while he directed Colt's and Champion's buying of provisions and beef cattle in advance of the inevitable price increases that followed the suspension of price-fixing. Wadsworth's concentration upon Connecticut in this successful maneuver attested eloquently to that state's central position in the supply of meat to the armies. The droves of beeves that Champion sent to Valley Forge on the eve of Philadelphia's evacuation kept Washington's army adequately supplied during the Monmouth campaign, while flour collected from Pennsylvania and New Jersey supplied bread. When Washington's army encamped in Westchester County before the British lines defending New York, Wadsworth grazed reserve herds of beef cattle in pastures on a twenty-mile radius, while establishing flour magazines at Headquarters and Peekskill in New York and at Sharon, Connecticut. The latter was stocked with Litchfield County flour, as well as with flour from Dutchess County, New York.

The major military operation of the late summer of 1778 was the allied attack upon British-held Newport. In this, the French fleet of the Comte d'Estaing cooperated with Major General John Sullivan's army, which was reinforced by a Continental contingent under Greene and New England militia including regiments from Connecticut. Congress's Marine Committee made Wadsworth responsible for supplying d'Estaing's fleet. But the Marine Committee, the Board of Treasury, and individual delegates to Congress interfered with his department's performance of this work with unfortunate results. Although salt provisions were scarce because of the Commissary of Issue's failure to put them up during the preceding winter, Champion supplied d'Estaing adequately with fresh meat. Bread was another matter. D'Estaing required the best quality of flour, of which there was a limited supply. Wadsworth might have filled this requirement, had Congress cooperated. Instead, and despite his objections, the Marine Committee required that bread for d'Estaing be baked in Philadelphia, and that it be carted from there to

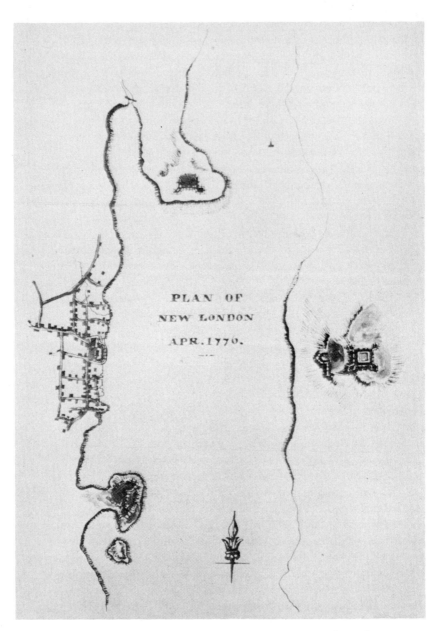

1776 map of New London. Benedict Arnold led a 1781 raid on the town to destroy American provisions. Fort Trumbull is on the lower left, Fort Griswold is on the right, and batteries are located at the top on Winthrop's Neck and on the town's waterfront. From Louis F. Middlebrook, *Maritime Connecticut During the American Revolution, 1775–1783*, Volume I.

Providence for delivery to the French fleet off Newport. This tied up innumerable quartermaster wagon trains with light loads of bread that molded en route, whereas they might have been better employed in carrying flour from Sharon to d'Estaing and to Sullivan's Providence magazine.

In mid-July, foreseeing a probable flour shortage at Providence, Wadsworth asked Congress secretly for permission to buy 20,000 barrels in Virginia and ship it in vessels to New England ports while d'Estaing controlled the sea. The congressional committee to which this urgent request was referred delayed reporting for a month, while Congressman Samuel Chase of Maryland, who was privy to the secret, organized a coterie that promptly bought up the available supply of flour, taking advantage of the wheat crop failure in Virginia and the partial failure in Maryland caused by the Hessian fly. Only Wadsworth's personal visit to Philadelphia wangled belated permission from Congress to make the desired purchase, but the Marine Committee assigned an inadequate convoy of but two warships for the flour vessels. After Wadsworth placed secret orders for 20,000 barrels with Colonel John Fitzgerald of Alexandria, Virginia, that individual, and Wadsworth himself at Baltimore, found that the supply was held entirely by the speculators. Meanwhile, d'Estaing's fleet had been severely damaged by a storm during a battle with the British fleet and had gone to Boston to refit, thus surrendering control of the sea off the coast of the northern states. Wadsworth's attempt to supply d'Estaing and Sullivan with Virginia flour and to establish New England flour magazines for future needs was thus defeated. And d'Estaing, denied the three months' supply that he demanded in Boston, employed a private merchant, one Price, who promptly paid such unprecedentedly high prices for flour and provisions as to disrupt the Commissary of Purchase's procurement in Massachusetts and upstate New York. It was, however, Wadsworth's organization which was primarily responsible for supplying d'Estaing so that he could sail to the West Indies.

Sullivan, meanwhile, had been supplied with difficulty during his attack upon Newport Island. To make up an adequate supply of provisions, in addition to what Colt could send from Connecticut, he secured state-owned provisions from Governor Trumbull, seized those held for the Continental Navy at New London, and borrowed more provisions from the Board of War at Boston. Champion supplied him with ample fresh meat. Colt managed to provide Sullivan sparingly with flour and other items from Connecticut. Sullivan's incompetent deputy of issues, however, misinformed Colt after the evacuation of Newport Island by telling him that he possessed sufficient flour. Then, suddenly, in early November that same official told Sullivan that the supply had been exhausted. Meanwhile, Congress's failure to provide Wadsworth with sufficient funds had obliged Colt's purchasers in Dutchess County to forfeit

West view of East Haddam Landing.

East Haddam Landing, one of many Connecticut river communities that were avenues for shipping supplies to the Continental Army. From John W. Barber, *Connecticut Historical Collections.*

contracts for more than 4,000 barrels. Lacking the flour that Wadsworth had sought to ship from Chesapeake Bay, Colt had to send flour to Providence from Sharon by slow ox cart trains. Since ice on the roads during an early severe winter interfered, at one time 1,000 barrels were held up for three weeks. More than once during that winter, Sullivan's furious troops lacked bread.

Colt, furthermore, was obliged also to provide flour for the garrison at Boston, the Hudson River command holding the forts of the Highlands, and the "Convention Troops" of Burgoyne's former army that were being held prisoners in eastern Massachusetts. Buying every barrel of available flour, frequently after seizure under Connecticut law, to satisfy such needs, Colt's Eastern Department diverted a critical supply from civilian channels. The situation was made worse when wheat and flour stocks were held off the market by merchants and farmers who anticipated a rise in price. Even before the war, Connecticut had never been able to fully satisfy the needs of Rhode Island and Massachusetts, which had imported large quantities of flour from New York, Pennsylvania, and Maryland. Now, cut off by sea from those sources, while the Virginia and Maryland crop failures greatly limited the total supply, and with the Connecticut flour surplus reduced much below 1774 levels, the Massachusetts and Rhode Island civilian populations experienced a flour famine of serious proportions.

Although Governor Trumbull issued 39 permits allowing Massachusetts merchants to buy limited amounts of flour in Connecticut for their towns, the flour price in Boston rose to 80s. per cwt. Providence had none at any price. The New York legislature at Poughkeepsie issued numerous permits allowing the export of flour from that state to Boston. Despite all that, thousands of civilians in New England suffered severely for months for lack of bread made from wheat flour and made out with limited supplies of rye bread and corn bread.

During that winter, especially in Connecticut, under Wadsworth's direction, Colt organized large-scale packing of salt pork and salt beef. Lesser quantities of these indispensable provisions were put up at Albany by deputy Jacob Cuyler. In the Middle and Southern Departments, a similar operation was carried on by deputies Blaine and William Aylett. To provide the indispensable salt for the great operation in the Eastern Department, Colt had imported it from Spain and the West Indies on a large scale, and shared a portion of this with Cuyler. Private importers also provided Blaine and Aylett with the necessary salt, and because of their efforts, great provisions magazines were established in New England, at Albany, and in the Middle States.

Meanwhile, in order to provide the armed forces with sufficient flour, Wadsworth went to Hartford after directing Aylett's purchase of a large quantity from Carter Braxton in Virginia, and after ordering Blaine to buy every available barrel in the Middle Department. From

A portion of Epaphoditus Champion's account book listing cattle purchased in 1778 for the Continental Army. From manuscript account book, Connecticut State Library.

Hartford, Wadsworth directed a secret service that identified the flour smugglers along the New York border, and this enabled him to seize much smuggled flour under New England state laws. He also seized privately-held flour in Connecticut as it moved in wagons along the roads. Then, as warm weather approached in the spring of 1779, the speculators began to unload their holdings in Pennsylvania and Maryland. Blaine bought sufficient flour in those states to tide the armed forces over until the next harvest. By the narrowest of margins, with regrettable lapses affecting Sullivan's Providence command owing in part again to its incompetent deputy of issues, Wadsworth succeeded in supplying the armed forces, including warships based in New London, with flour. This was accomplished despite the diversion of much flour to the French West Indies fleet on the insistence of John Holker, French naval agent at Philadelphia.

Connecticut figured not at all in the supply of the three successful expeditions against the Iroquois during the summer of 1779. In October, however, it appeared that d'Estaing's West Indies fleet would come up for a joint operation against New York at a time when Congress's financial stringency impeded Commissary of Purchases procurement and a severe drought stopped the operation of many New York flour mills. Wadsworth asked Governor Trumbull for a state law similar to that of New York which would reserve a portion of Connecticut's wheat crop for the army. The General Assembly declined to pass the measure. Instead, it voted wheat conditionally for such state militia as might be called out to reinforce Washington for the combined operation. That attack on New York, however, never occurred. Then, when desperate for flour in early November, Wadsworth came to Hartford to plead for a grant of the conditional wheat, the governor and Council denied his request. Instead, they recommended that his department exchange its salt and West India goods in Connecticut for flour. Needing the salt on hand for winter meat-packing and all the rum he could get to supply the thirsty armies, Wadsworth angrily declined to venture upon so impracticable a scheme.

He was even more infuriated by Congress's refusal to enable him to take the large amount of West India rum captured by Commodore Whipple from the Jamaica fleet and brought into Boston, and to barter it with New York farmers for wheat. Congress's Committee of Supervision of the supply departments had also ignored Wadsworth's recommendations and interfered with his administration, while the Board of Treasury failed to provide sufficient funds. Certain that Congress lacked confidence in him, Wadsworth resigned, effective December 31, 1779, although President Samuel Huntington, chairman Jesse Root of the Committee of Supervision, and General Washington urged him to remain in office. Wadsworth was also furious at bitter but ill-considered criticism of the Commissary of Purchases and the Quartermaster Department

COLONEL JEREMIAH WADSWORTH.

Jeremiah Wadsworth, who during 1778 and 1779, served as the Continental Commissary General. From Henry Greenleaf Pearson, *James S. Wadsworth of Geneseo* (1913).

which attributed to them responsibility for the inflationary price spiral. Better judgment would have attributed it to Congress's attempt to finance the war by currency inflation.

Then, on September 20th, Congress resolved to emit no more than $200,000,000 in currency, a figure that was reached within a month. Refused additional funds, Wadsworth's department bought necessary supplies on credit in Connecticut and elsewhere. By January 1st it had incurred a debt of $22,000,000 (at 40 to 1, equal to approximately $440,000 in specie). When the new year dawned, the Commissary of Purchases' credit was destroyed when Wadsworth succeeded in getting Congress to pay only $6,000,000 of the debt. Congress, however, had resolved to disband that department with its national system of procurement and supply of the armed forces in favor of a new system which it had adopted in December. Meanwhile, following Wadsworth's retirement, Colt and Champion also resigned. This terminated Connecticut's influential role in the direction of the supply of the Continental Army and Navy.

From July, 1775, until December, 1779, *official* Connecticut did not figure importantly, as we have seen, in the supply of the Continental armed forces. Occasionally the state's reserve of provisions was lent to Peter Colt, Deputy Commissary General of Purchases of the Eastern Department. On one occasion, it was sold to General Sullivan during the Newport expedition of 1778. State seizure laws enabled the commissaries, with the cooperation of county sheriffs and town selectmen, to requisition foods engrossed by speculators or hoarded and withheld from market by farmers. The state embargo, extended and tightened by the General Assembly from year to year until 1780, created an artificial surplus available to purchasing commissaries and quartermasters. In May, 1777, during a temporary shortage of West India goods and clothing among the Connecticut Line regiments at Peekskill, the General Assembly had appointed Elijah Hubbard Commissary and Superintendent of Supplies and Refreshments. He was directed to take a wagon load of these articles to each battalion of Connecticut troops in service and also to those being recruited. Such a small supplement had been only incidental to the daily supply of those troops, responsibility for which resided then in Joseph Trumbull's Commissary Department. Apart from these measures, Connecticut's contribution to the provisioning of the armed forces during those four and a half years had been made by individual farmers, cattle feeders, millers, merchants, and other suppliers as they responded to the offers of the purchasing commissaries and quartermasters to buy their food, drink, salt, forage, livestock, and draft oxen and carts.

Connecticut's responsibility *as a state* for supplying the Continental forces began in December, 1779, when Congress abandoned the policy of supplying them via national supply services functioning as staff departments of the army under Washington's command. This began on December 11, when Congress requisitioned 8,000 barrels of flour from Connecticut, one of six states from which it demanded flour or corn for the army. Virginia, because of a second wheat crop failure, was asked for only 20,000 barrels of corn, and Maryland, a great flour state, for only 15,000 barrels of flour. In reply to Congress's request, Governor Trumbull asserted that Connecticut lacked a substantial surplus of flour, and the governor, consequently, ignored the requisition.

Within a month, however, Congress skeletonized the Commissary of Purchases. Under the new Commissary General of Purchases, Ephraim Blaine, it was left with the function of receiving supplies from the states from which were to be requisitioned specific quotas, with interim authority to buy supplies in states which should reject their quotas. Weeks of bargaining between state delegations in Congress delayed adoption of yearly quotas (subject to variation as the campaign progressed) until February 25, 1780. The initial delivery date was postponed until April 1. In each state accepting its quota, the Commissary of Purchases and Quartermaster Department would stop purchasing, as it, by implication, would set up its own organization to procure the required supplies.

Connecticut's role as the leading provisions state became clear when Congress assigned to it the leading beef and pork quota of 78,400,000 pounds. Massachusetts with a quota of 56,000,000, North Carolina with nearly fifty million, and Virginia with 47,000,000 came next. Connecticut ranged fourth in rum, with a quota of 68,550 gallons, behind Massachusetts, South Carolina, and Virginia. Connecticut's salt quota of 1,011 tons was eighth on the list. Its hay quota of 500 tons was the same as that of New York and Delaware, and much below the quotas assigned to New Jersey and Pennsylvania. No additional flour quota was levied on Connecticut, this article being drawn entirely from the Middle States and upper South. Connecticut's onion crop was ignored, although Wadsworth had had Governor Trumbull reserve it entirely for the Continental Army in 1778.

Initially, in February, 1780, the Connecticut General Assembly refused to accept the state quota or to cooperate with Blaine. Despite ample evidence of great suffering in the Continental Army, Governor Trumbull refused to appoint a state deputy to serve under him, and declined to expend the $200,000 that the desperate Congress had sent to him for the purchase of supplies. The governor and the Connecticut legislature were furious at Congress's jettisoning of the national supply services. Hence, they delayed action until late April. Congress's stiff prodding at that time persuaded the General Assembly to accept the quota, to appoint a state commissary to procure the necessary supplies, and to appropriate the beggarly sum of £6,000 in new state currency to finance their procurement.

During the interim, the armies experienced their worst suffering of the entire war. Washington collected what supplies he could by forced contributions levied on inhabitants in areas around the several winter quarters and posts. The commandant on the Hudson, Major General Robert Howe, pleaded with Jeremiah Wadsworth, now a private citizen at Hartford, to save the armies from starving. Expending his own funds and what he could squeeze from Blaine's organization, Wadsworth energetically collected provisions, beef cattle, and other supplies and dispatched them to the armies. What he sent probably prevented absolute starvation in the Hudson River command, and it alleviated somewhat the plight of Washington's army at Morristown until the states' quotas of supplies began belatedly to trickle in.

In Connecticut, the General Assembly had created a divided state commissariat, over which Colonel Henry Champion, Chief Purchasing Commissary, exercised general supervision. Captain James Watson of Windsor, however, was given charge of buying rum and hay. Champion delegated to him responsibility for buying flour, and retained for himself the procuring of beef cattle and provisions. Captain Henry Champion, Jr., was appointed receiver of Connecticut's Continental supplies for Commissary General of Purchases Blaine. The senior Champion's work, however, was complicated by Blaine's order of late July that Champion divert a third of all beef procured to supply the French expedition that had landed at Newport.

The system of specific supplies, as the new program was known, rested upon Congress's assumption that the states collectively were to supply the armed forces adequately from current resources. This implied that each state would tax its citizens sufficiently to enable it to buy and ship its quota of supplies, finance its own government and militia call-outs, and pay the money quota that Congress levied on it (but from which the cost of its supply quota, if filled, was deductible). Connecticut's commissary, incidentally, was financed by paying its officials two per cent commission on purchases. The basic assumption upon which the system of specific supplies rested, however, was fallacious. No country has ever been able to finance a major war solely from current resources and revenues. The loose confederation of the United States during 1780–1781 was no exception, and all the states failed to fill their supply quotas.

In June, 1780, Colonel Henry Champion informed Governor Trumbull that he had sent several herds of forty beef cattle each to Washington's army and had on hand 100 more "tolerable" beeves ready for shipment. He had also sent from Massachusetts two or three herds bought with Continental currency supplied to him by Blaine as his deputy. For several months he had been able to buy more cattle in Massachusetts than in Connecticut. Although he would continue every exertion, Champion said, all the cattle that he had on the road were insufficient "for ye

Epaphoditus Champion, the son of Commissary Henry Champion, was active in obtaining provisions in Connecticut for Continental troops. From Francis Bacon Trowbridge, *The Champion Genealogy* (1891).

absolute necessity of the troops," and he was obliged in great measure to neglect the Hudson River command in the Highlands. When Champion's herds arrived at Washington's camp in New Jersey they improved its supply situation temporarily.

Governor Trumbull did not have to be told by Champion why he found it difficult to procure beef cattle in Connecticut. It was simply impossible to buy them on credit. Furthermore, the large cattle feeding industry that had formerly marketed its fat beeves to Champion during 1775–1779 had been wrecked by Congress's refusal to pay more than half of Champion's large debts to the cattle feeders. By March 1, 1780, his total debt has risen to more than £2,400,000. The cattle feeders now found themselves without funds either to buy lean cattle for feeding or to pay for corn for that purpose. Furthermore, during January–April, 1780, when Connecticut rejected its supply quota, there was no military market in Connecticut for fat cattle. Embittered cattle feeders threatened to sue Champion and his purchasing commissaries for their beef debts. Wadsworth bought many of these debts to prevent such suits, and joined the cattle feeders in petitioning the General Assembly for relief. Finally, in May, 1781, he secured for them payment in state certificates of the specie value of their claims, payable in specie a year after the war should end. Meanwhile, however, cattle feeders lacked the means and also the inclination to fatten cattle on a large scale. The supply of superior beeves available to Champion as Senior Purchasing Commissary for filling the state quota was, therefore, much reduced.

Yet, Connecticut at that time, when properly led, was capable of accepting the obligation to supply the army quickly and adequately. In May, Jeremiah Wadsworth attended the General Assembly as the spokesman of the merchants and of all who desired full support of the war effort. Washington, on June 2, asked for Wadsworth's personal intervention with Governor Trumbull to secure immediately a large shipment of provisions from Connecticut to West Point to enable it to resist an expected, up-river attack from New York by General Henry Clinton. Simultaneously, in a revision of Connecticut's quota under the system of specific supplies, General Philip Schuyler's Committee on Cooperation at Washington's headquarters requisitioned a long list of items. These, Washington stated, were absolutely essential. Wadsworth exhibited the Commander in Chief's letter, together with letters from Generals Greene and Jedediah Huntington describing the semi-starvation of the army and its great weakness, to legislative committees.

So informed, Governor Trumbull ordered the provisions sent to West Point. Led by Wadsworth, the General Assembly voted funds to Nehemiah Hubbard, Jr., Deputy Quartermaster General, to finance their transportation by his wagon trains. The legislature voted a heavy tax and also an emission of £100,000 in state currency. Of this sum, £20,000 was promptly lent to the Comte de Rochambeau's *Commissaire de Guerre*, Ashir de Corny, to enable him to buy supplies and horses in the state in preparation for the landing of the French expedition.

Of much greater importance, however, was the legislature's acceptance of the Schuyler committee's requisition for 2,520 rank and file of militia, properly armed and officered in five regiments, to rendezvous at Danbury in July. The requisition also demanded: for each month through September, 1,500 barrels of flour, 666,035 pounds of beef, 100 hogsheads of rum, 500 bushels of salt, 30,000 pounds of bacon, and 9,142 bushels of grain for forage, plus 100 ox carts with 400 oxen properly yoked and equipped, and 1,000 draft horses to be delivered on July 1st with the ox cart train. This accepted requisition revised Connecticut's yearly quota of February 25th drastically by scaling down the beef quota, adding flour and grain, more than doubling the hay, and including the draft horses and ox cart train. However, Chief Commissary Champion's work was simplified, since deliveries were put on a monthly basis.

After the General Assembly's acceptance of the revised state quota, what was needed was adequate procurement by the state commissary with concomitant delivery of supplies, the ox cart train, and the horses to the army. The actual performance fell far below the requisition's requirements. Wadsworth's energies, as Wadsworth was the most interested legislator, were diverted to supplying Rochambeau's army as the unpaid agent of de Corny. In doing so he employed the services of the state commissary, diverting flour, beef cattle, sheep, and forage to Newport. Blaine's order to Colonel Champion actually authorized diversion of a third of the beef cattle procured for Washington's army to Rochambeau. For inexplicable reasons, Colonel Champion and Captain Watson, the leading state commissaries, were under-financed by the state government, while they and their aides spent only a part of their time in supplying the American army.

Champion's initial deliveries to Washington's camp in the early summer had alleviated its troops' condition. But by August 22 they were again subsisting without meat. Washington appealed to Governor Trumbull for an immediate supply. Trumbull and the Council of Safety promptly informed Colonel Champion that Washington must have beef. Champion replied to them bluntly that nothing could be done without money, and he probably told them of how he had supplied cattle and sheep to Rochambeau when supplied with ready money by Wadsworth.

By that time, Rochambeau had turned to private contractors for his army's supply. These contractors dispensed French coin and French army bills of exchange in payment for livestock, flour, grain, etc., and this gold, silver, and highly-respected paper appealed much more to farmers and merchants than did the limited quantity of state currency that Champion's purchasers offered in Connecticut, or than did the Continental currency which Massachusetts state purchasers offered farther north.

Probably Champion's staff and Governor Trumbull and his Council of safety were aware, by mid-August, that the Schuyler committee requisitions, made with authority delegated by Congress, had been levied disproportionately upon Connecticut. That state and Massachusetts tied for first place among the states in the beef and pork monthly quota of 666,035 pounds. Connecticut ranked second in bacon, third in rum, flour, grain, and horses. And Connecticut was the only state required to provide an ox cart train for Washington's army. Unfair as this disproportionate requisition upon Connecticut may have been, it certainly gave full recognition to its reputation as "the provisions state." But realization of the quota's unfairness could hardly have provided adequate motivation for full compliance.

Furthermore, during July to September, Connecticut militia served at Newport under Major General William Heath, cooperating with Rochambeau in defense of that island against a threatened British attack. Other militia were mustered at threatened Shore points when a great British fleet of warships and transports appeared in western Long Island Sound. Much of the foodstuffs that Champion procured had to be diverted to supplying these militia regiments on duty.

For whatever reasons, Connecticut lagged steadily in filling its monthly quotas of supplies for the Continental Army. As all the states did so, Commissary General of Purchases Blaine informed Congress bluntly in August, 1780, that the system of specific supplies was a failure, and that the supply situation of the armies was most precarious. As the condition of Washington's army worsened in September, the General wrote to Governor Trumbull that as a part of Connecticut's deficiency in meeting its supply quota, no cattle from Champion had arrived in five weeks. Not having raised sufficient revenue to finance Champion's procurement for the American forces, Connecticut was inevitably delinquent. The fault, the governor informed Roger Sherman in Congress, lay in the system of specific supplies. Washington denounced the system to Congress as "the most uncertain, expensive, and injurious that could be devised." On September 22 at Hartford, Governor Trumbull told Washington that very few beef cattle could be expected from Connecticut.

Unwilling to tax war-weary Connecticut to pay for the state's quota of supplies, although it was experiencing the flush of prosperity as the result of French military and naval procurement, and as crops and livestock were then plentiful, the General Assembly adopted a supply act in October, 1780. This law required that each town in the state furnish beef, pork, and wheat flour to the value of five pence per pound of assessed valuation for taxation. The beef was to be delivered on December

15, the pork and flour on January 15, with 200 per cent penalty for delinquency. In November, the legislature raised this so-called "beef tax" to six pence on the pound. Champion was appointed to receive it and ordered to forward the proceeds to the Continental Army. The result in paid-in cattle, however, was insufficient to enable Connecticut to fill the unrealistically high weekly quota of 539 beef cattle which Congress had adopted on September 15. Although Massachusetts' quota was but 395 beeves, that state, instead of Connecticut, had become Blaine's chief source of beef. In Connecticut, instead of a state-directed program of packing salt provisions, such work was left to the discretion of private citizens, since in paying the "beef tax" they could substitute salt meat for beef cattle. Yet, if a large quantity of provisions had been packed on state account and delivered to Washington, his troops could have consumed them instead of fresh meat during the winter and spring until grass-fed cattle became available. Wadsworth, the state's genius in logistics, was now unfortunately fully occupied as Rochambeau's Agent.

It was not surprising, therefore, that on January 19, 1781, Washington warned Governor Trumbull that if Connecticut's monthly quota of beef cattle were not delivered regularly, he could not be responsible for garrisoning the Hudson River forts and the posts on Long Island Sound, or for maintaining even a single regiment in the field.

On April 10, 1781, with his army again on the brink of starvation, Washington wrote to Governor Trumbull that only salt provisions from Connecticut could relieve it. The Council ordered the salt meat collected under the October, 1780, supply act to be delivered to Deputy Quartermaster General Ralph Pomeroy. In May, Washington sent Major General William Heath, his second in command, to present the army's needs to Connecticut's General Assembly. In response to his plea for beef and rum, the legislature ordered 1,000 barrels of salt meat and twenty hogsheads of rum sent immediately, appropriating £3,000 to pay the cost of transportation. Only £2,000, however, was voted to Champion for immediate purchase of beef for the army. The towns west of the Connecticut River were ordered to procure teams and transport the provisions collected under the October, 1780, act to Fishkill on the Hudson. On May 15, Heath wrote to Washington that 160 cattle were being forwarded immediately. Many of these were consumed undoubtedly at the Hudson River outposts, since few reached Washington's army. There was hope, however, since in April a New England inter-state meeting at Providence had adopted a schedule for these states' deliveries of supplies.

Yet Washington's army during the early summer of 1781, before and after Rochambeau's army joined it on the Hudson on July 5, was seriously deficient in supplies. A few days later, Washington reported to Governor Trumbull that since May 12 the following number of cattle had been received by his headquarters: from Massachusetts, 230; from

New Hampshire, 30; and from Connecticut, 52. Connecticut's contribution to the war effort that summer was at a low ebb. For 1780–1781, of Senior Purchasing Commissary Champion's total expenditures of £99,000 in specie, only $156,000 of this had bought supplies sent to the Continental armies. James Watson may have expended half as much again for flour, hay, and rum. The total expenditure had fallen far short of what was required for fulfillment of the state's supply quotas under the system of specific supplies. It was this failure in performance that justified Washington's repeated but vain appeals to Governor Trumbull for the food which Connecticut had promised to feed his army. Late in 1781, Superintendent of Finance Robert Morris resorted to contracting in order to supply it, a step that relieved Connecticut of further responsibility.

During 1780–1781, while Connecticut as a state was faltering so gravely in supplying the Continental Army under the system of specific supplies, its citizens were contributing notably to the supply of the French expedition commanded by the Comte de Rochambeau. Although some of this would have occurred in any case as long as the Comte's army was situated at Newport, the Connecticut contribution to its supply was greatly enhanced by the central role played in it by Jeremiah Wadsworth of Hartford.

Wadsworth's involvement in the supply of Rochambeau's army began at Hartford in late April, 1780, when the Marquis de Lafayette, returning from France to his position in the Continental Army, introduced to him Ashir de Corny, the commissary whom Rochambeau had sent in advance to collect supplies in preparation for his expedition's arrival. Lafayette extracted a pledge from Wadsworth that he would assist de Corny, who knew little of the actual conditions that governed procurement of supplies in the United States. Wadsworth, however, stipulated that he receive no compensation from de Corny so that his motives for assisting him would not be questioned. Then, when Lafayette presented de Corny to Congress at Philadelphia, Congress asked Connecticut to assist him in supplying Rochambeau.

When de Corny returned to Hartford on June 22 while the General Assembly was in session, he requested a loan of £20,000. Wadsworth and the governor arranged the loan, but Wadsworth refused to contract. He did, however, agree to serve as de Corny's unpaid agent in collecting the necessary supplies, probably after receiving Governor Trumbull's promise that the state commissary would assist him. Since the governor told de Corny that he approved, the French officials believed that Wadsworth had been appointed the state official responsible for assisting him and that Connecticut's state government was pledged to supply him. De Corny assigned to Wadsworth the £20,000 loan and also the coin and French bills that French Minister, the Chevalier de la Luzerne, had sent earlier to Thomas Mumford. He gave Wadsworth detailed orders, and left for Newport, confident that all needed supplies would be delivered there before Rochambeau arrived. Wadsworth, who spoke little French, had tried to explain to de Corny, who spoke no English, the difficulties confronting their procurement so quickly in a state exhausted by a long war, and had declared that any failure would not be due to his lack of activity. Wadsworth regarded himself as a private citizen who was voluntarily helping the French, America's allies, and he knew that he did not represent the state government, although he could rely upon Colonel Champion and Captain Watson to assist him in collecting the supplies.

Wadsworth quickly recruited purchasers and sent his former Headquarters Assistant, Royal Flint, to Newport to assist de Corny. Beginning procurement immediately, Wadsworth ordered Colonel Champion to deliver beef cattle and sheep to Newport, where Rochambeau was expected. Treasurer Lawrence, however, did not hand him the £20,000 in state currency until July 5. It took time to collect flour, grain, cider, provisions, and linseed oil, load them on vessels, and get the latter to Newport, just as it did to buy and drive horses and Champion's herds to that island. On July 8, Wadsworth began negotiations for cattle with the Massachusetts Committee of Supplies that furnished the Continental Army. Simultaneously, he asked General Schuyler's Committee on Cooperation at Washington's headquarters to arrange such a collaboration with de Corny that procurement for the French would not interfere with the supply of the Continental Army by the states. A carefully coordinated system of supply, said Wadsworth, was necessary if the American army were not to suffer. With most of the committee ill, and lacking authority to arrange such matters himself, Schuyler asked General Greene to inform Wadsworth that he must supply the French in the most effective manner without regard to the states.

Rochambeau landed at Newport on July 11 to find only three days' supplies on hand to provision his army and convoying squadron. When reprimanded by Rochambeau, the embarrassed de Corny attributed the shortage to the failure of Wadsworth, as Connecticut's supposed agent, to keep promises that de Corny thought he had made to have ample supplies delivered at Newport in advance of Rochambeau's arrival. Reproached in turn by de Corny for *his* failure, Wadsworth prodded his assistants and Champion to redoubled efforts. At the same time, however, Wadsworth resigned as de Corny's agent, since he could not, as a former Commissary General of Purchases, suffer himself to be reprimanded by a mere French *commissaire de guerre*. In the interval before his resignation was accepted on July 27, Wadsworth forwarded more supplies and provided for hundreds of Pennsylvania horses and wagon teams that Luzerne had purchased and sent to Rochambeau during their passage through Connecticut. Since Wadsworth's expenditures for de Corny totalled more than £17,000 in specie, it is evident that his short-lived supply of Rochambeau as de Corny's agent had been substantial. Practically all of this sum had been expended in Connecticut.

Even before accepting Wadsworth's resignation, Rochambeau's *intendant*, the Chevalier de la Tarlé, began to contract with private enterprisers for the French army's supply. Wadsworth, when invited by Tarlé to contract, declined. Tarlé's contractors drew upon Rhode Island, Connecticut, and Massachusetts for supplies, paying for them with French coin and French army bills. This interfered seriously with procurement for the American armed forces by state commissaries, who could only compete with the unpopular, greatly-depreciated Continental currency or the slightly-depreciated Connecticut state currency. Congress failed to negotiate with Rochambeau, as Wadsworth had recommended, a coordinated system for supplying the armed forces, although it did ask the French general to buy supplies with Continental currency alone.

As a result of the grave damage done to procurement of the state quotas for General Washington, Massachusetts sent commissioners to inquire of Rochambeau if he would accept an interstate system of supply. He consented, on condition that it would not interfere with his existing contracts, and that he receive supplies from the states at their first cost. Simultaneously, Tarlé offered to contract exclusively with the State of Massachusetts for the French army's supply. The Massachusetts commissioners sent the record of their negotiation with Rochambeau to Governor Trumbull. Trumbull and his Council of Safety appointed three commissioners, including Wadsworth, who were directed to meet with those from the other eastern states and negotiate a method of supplying Rochambeau that would not conflict with the supply of the Continental Army or with Connecticut's laws. What Trumbull and his Council sought, obviously, was the imposition upon Rochambeau of the same system of specific supplies, on a regional basis, that was keeping American troops in a chronic condition of semi-starvation.

Rochambeau was quick to comprehend this. He had certainly seen the imperfections in the system of specific supplies. After he had first landed at Newport, he had been reinforced with New England militia and some Continental troops commanded by General Heath. But the New England states supplied Heath's force of some 5,000 men so poorly that in order to feed them, the general was obliged to borrow flour, provisions, and other supplies repeatedly from Rochambeau's magazines. Although he was dissatisfied with the poor calibre and the performance of Tarlé's contractors, Rochambeau did not intend to subject his men to the system of supply that had nearly starved Heath's troops.

While he was Wadsworth's guest at Hartford on September 20–22 during his conference with General Washington, Rochambeau learned from him and Lafayette of the former Commissary General of Purchase's brilliant record in logistics. Simultaneously, Rochambeau learned from Governor Trumbull that Wadsworth was delegated to join in imposing on the French expedition a regional system of specific supplies. Then Rochambeau returned to Newport to learn that the Massachusetts Council would not contract to supply him.

In early October, Wadsworth, as Connecticut's agent, appeared at Newport to collect the state's loan to de Corny and to settle his personal account as de Corny's unpaid agent. In a deft maneuver to avoid having imposed on the French forces the contemplated regional system of specific supplies, Tarlé, Rochambeau, and his senior officers invited and urged Wadsworth to become their exclusive agent for supplying the French army on a commission of five per cent on purchases. Again, the problem of communication arose. The reluctant Wadsworth spoke little French, Rochambeau spoke no English, and Tarlé did business in French. As he gave way to the French officers' flattering insistence, Wadsworth took as his partner one of Tarlé's contractors, the French-speaking Englishman, John Carter, who was General Schuyler's son-in-law.

Wadsworth returned to Connecticut as Rochambeau's agent, but he promised Governor Trumbull that he would minimize the conflict between French procurement and the system of specific supplies. Wadsworth persuaded Trumbull and the Council of Safety, of which he was a member, to approve of his agency and to exclude Tarlé's beef cattle contractors from Connecticut. This forced Tarlé to terminate their contract on November 1. Wadsworth helped Carter to complete his contracts, and then the partners assumed sole charge of supplying the French army with food, drink, salt, forage, and firewood. Stationed at Newport, Carter was the partnership's liaison in daily touch with Tarlé. At Hartford, Wadsworth quickly perfected an organization of purchasers and chartered vessels that enabled him to send a stream of supplies to Newport. Carter did some buying in Rhode Island, and he also negotiated a contract for hay with a Massachusetts firm. When the Massachusetts people welshed on the contract, the embarrassed partners then sent Peter Colt, one of Wadsworth's assistants, to western Connecticut for the urgently-needed supply. When firewood deliveries from Fisher's Island and eastern Connecticut lagged, Carter persuaded Admiral Chevalier de Ternay to detach ten of his ships to bring in the 800 cords required.

After sending one more drove of cattle to Newport, Colonel Champion delegated that business to his sons, Henry, Jr., and Epaphroditus. Then, when a combination of cattle speculators threatened to raise the price of beeves for the French during the winter, Wadsworth persuaded Tarlé to allow him to contract in advance in low coin prices for the entire winter's supply, including enough cattle to enable the French commissary to pack a large supply of salt beef. With Tarlé's order for increased weekly beef-cattle deliveries in hand, Wadsworth thus revived the military market in Connecticut for fat cattle and restored the cattle feeding business to something like its former volume and prosperity.

From the beginning of Wadsworth and Carter's operations, however, Rochambeau expected them to expend only Continental currency in procurement, as Congress requested. John Holker, now French Consul at Philadelphia, and Luzerne purchased millions in currency by selling bills of exchange on France, and Monsieur de Baulny, Treasurer of Rochambeau's army, secured more currency by marketing French army bills in Boston. Exclusive procurement with Continental currency would minimize interference with state commissaries' procurement for the Continental Army, although competitive bidding for supplies would still persist. But the precedent set earlier by Tarlé's contractors who had paid coin and French bills for supplies, the farmers' insistence upon being paid in coin for hay and grain, and the cattle feeders' demand for coin in payment for fat cattle, obliged Wadsworth and Carter to insist upon being supplied with much coin and French bills in addition to currency. In practice, however, although it resulted in paying more for supplies, Tarlé advanced to the partners much Continental currency and a large number of French bills at a discount, plus a little coin. Coin, however, *was* paid for the winter's contract beef cattle, some £11,000 in early March of 1781. Also, £3,216 more in coin was paid to the Champions for cattle, sheep, and hogs delivered to the French between May 7 and July 2. To secure coin for other procurement, which they paid out in combination with currency and French bills to suppliers, Wadsworth and Carter regularly sold French bills for coin at increasing discounts at Boston.

Despite his approval of Wadsworth's private agency, Governor Trumbull, for the four New England states, invited Rochambeau in late December to accept supply by them instead. Replying on January 1, 1781, Rochambeau stated that he was perfectly satisfied with Wadsworth's agency, which he greatly preferred to the system which had obliged him to lend supplies repeatedly to General Heath during the preceding six months.

But perhaps Governor Trumbull, too, was satisfied with the arrangement by which Jeremiah Wadsworth had been able to revive Connecticut's role as the provisions state. Nor were Wadsworth's dealings solely with Rochambeau. In addition, Major Grandchain of the French squadron at Newport contracted repeatedly with Wadsworth and Carter, and Wadsworth assisted him in negotiating for flour from Albany. Within a few months, Wadsworth had shipped to the French squadron from Connecticut £6,500 (specie) worth of supplies. And so successful was Wadsworth and Carter's procurement of supplies for the French in eastern Connecticut, that the New London area soon was virtually stripped of surplus food. Large shipments of cider from the Connecticut River valley, and the delivery of much cheese to the French army commissary supplemented the large quantities of Connecticut flour, salt pork, and hay, rye, oats, and corn for forage which Wadsworth's chartered vessels landed at the French wharves at Newport. Thus, Wadsworth and Carter's supply of the French expedition brought prosperity to farmers, cattle feeders, dairymen, and ship-owners in Connecticut between November 1, 1780, and June 20, 1781, when the French army left Providence on its march through Connecticut to rendezvous with Washington's army on the Hudson River.

In preparation for this march, Wadsworth, on Rochambeau's orders, contracted for a wagon train consisting of 205 ox-drawn wagons, with three yokes of oxen each, and twenty horse-drawn wagons, all to be driven by Connecticut drivers and directed by Connecticut conductors in brigades of ten wagons each. In addition, Wadsworth supplied Rochambeau with more than 500 horses, most of which were bought in Connecticut. Furthermore, Wadsworth and Carter had sole charge of supplying and moving the French artillery, for which more horses and horse-drawn wagons were necessary. Makers of large wagons such as Captain Frederick Cleveland of Pomfret, the farmers who hired their oxen in this manner to the French, and Connecticut's many horse breeders all profited from this procurement, while daily wages were earned by more than 275 Connecticut men in transporting the effects of the French army. To all of this must be added the profits of the wagon contract received by Nehemiah Hubbard, Jr., and Roger Bulkley and the salaries paid by Wadsworth and Carter to their assistants and clerical staff who also came from Connecticut. With good reason, the partners' supply of Rochambeau's army could well have been regarded as a Connecticut operation.

In addition to these preparations, on Rochambeau's orders, Wadsworth and Carter established ovens and a large flour magazine at Hartford at a cost of £5,919. These were to supply the French army on its march. At carefully-planned camp sites, forage and supplemental food was collected. These purchases helped to explain the enthusiasm with which the people of each area greeted the French army at each camp site and joined with its troops in dancing together to the music of the army's band. The £4,000 that Wadsworth and Carter expended to finance the march, although Rochambeau praised their economy to the French Minister of War, added that much more to Connecticut's prosperity.

While Rochambeau's army remained at Camp Phillipsburg on the Hudson from July 5 to August 15, 1781, Wadsworth and Carter continued to draw on Connecticut for supplies. Although the flour provided had been bought in the Albany area the preceding February and stored at Rhinebeck, the failure of Lewis, Parker, and Duer to fulfill their forage contract in New York obliged Wadsworth and Carter to rely unexpectedly upon western Connecticut for the grain and hay that prevented Rochambeau's livestock from starving to death in mid-summer. Wadsworth even shipped grain by water from Hartford to Stamford and had it carted overland to Camp Phillipsburg. Between July 5 and August 11, the Champion brothers delivered to the French army from Connecticut 927 fat oxen and 356 sheep, together worth £14,950 in coin.

To a limited extent, Connecticut also profited from Rochambeau's sudden march to Williamsburg, Virginia, to join in the siege of Yorktown. At the beginning of the march on August 17, Wadsworth drew upon the Danbury area for additional ox and horse teams and wagons. The enlarged wagon train accompanied the French army, the drivers, conductors, and contractors profiting accordingly. At Williamsburg, at the end of the march, Wadsworth and Carter paid the driver-owners for the large numbers of their oxen that were promptly eaten by the French troops there. More succulent beef was provided to them during the march, the siege of Yorktown, and for two months thereafter by herds of fat beeves driven by the Champion brothers all the way from Connecticut, at a total cost of over £13,000 in coin. All this explains why Connecticut Yankees were heard to yearn audibly during that autumn for the return of the French army.

When the French army returned to the Hudson River in early September, 1782, Wadsworth and Carter again drew upon Connecticut for a portion of its supplies. Connecticut provided all those needed for the army's march through the state in late October. Emergency shipments of Connecticut flour supported it while it waited at Providence for final repairs to Marquis de Vaudreuil's fleet at Boston. In December, the French sailed for the West Indies. Hartford profited, of course, when Wadsworth brought home afterward some £49,000 that he had earned from his agency for Rochambeau.

Wadsworth and Carter profited, also, from a seventy-six day emergency contract that they assumed at Robert Morris's urgent request for the supply of the main American army from October 15–December 31, 1781. The Superintendent of Finance had been unable to pay the cheating regular contractors, Comfort Sands & Company, on a monthly basis. In fulfilling the Wadsworth and Carter contract, Nehemiah Hubbard, Jr., was their administrative officer. Washington's troops were delighted when Wadsworth once more assumed responsibility for feeding them. Again, Connecticut was drawn upon for fat beeves, for a portion of the flour required, and for provisions and rum. Wadsworth's share of the profits on the contract was £5,500. After Duer and Parker contracted to supply Washington's army in 1783, Wadsworth and Carter secretly financed Phelps, Champion & Company, their beef cattle subcontractors who delivered Connecticut beef to a total value of some £15,000. Thus, from October 15, 1782, to the Continental Army's disbandment in 1784, Connecticut became again a major source of supplies for its maintenance.

It is evident from the foregoing narrative that Connecticut's role in supplying the American and French armies during the War of Independence was far greater than her small size and relatively small population would have suggested. In large part, this was owing to her commercial agriculture whose annual surpluses were reserved for military consumption by the state embargo on exports. But the great extent to which these surpluses were drawn upon to feed the Continental forces between 1775 and 1779, and then the French expedition between 1780 and 1782, was due to the logistical genius of Joseph Trumbull and Jeremiah Wadsworth, Connecticut men. Even while out of office, Wadsworth voluntarily supplied Gates' Saratoga campaign in 1777, and later he did the same for Howe's Highlands command in 1780. And Wadsworth's diversion of Connecticut food and forage to supply the French during 1780–1782, while the inept state government failed to supply Washington's army adequately under the system of specific supplies, indicates that the Connecticut merchants' skill in logistics was just as important in achieving the ultimate result as was Nature's bounty in a small agrarian state. What must be stressed is that during the first five years of the war, Connecticut held a central, vitally-important position in the interstate system of supply organized by the Commissary and the Commissary of Purchases departments, with which the state government cordially cooperated. Thereafter Connecticut's functioning as "The Provisions State" primarily served Rochambeau's expedition, and in this way contributed to the ultimate victory at Yorktown.

It is said that when Rochambeau and his army embarked for the West Indies, the officers and men gave a vote of thanks for American hospitality and expressed regret at their leaving. One cannot help but wonder whether these expansive sentiments might not have been composed while the Frenchmen were savoring the last of the Champion brothers' fat Connecticut beeves!

BIBLIOGRAPHICAL NOTE

The preceding narrative presents data that were derived from a wide range of primary sources, and secondary works. The most important manuscript collections drawn upon were the Jeremiah Wadsworth Papers, Henry Champion Papers, Jonathan Trumbull, Sr., Papers, and Joseph Trumbull Papers in the Connecticut Historical Society; the Trumbull Papers and the Connecticut Archives in the Connecticut State Library; the Jeremiah Wadsworth Papers in the Wadsworth Atheneum; the Jeremiah Wadsworth Papers in the New York Historical Society; the Chaloner and White Papers in the Historical Society of Pennsylvania; the Comte de Rochambeau Papers, James Wadsworth Papers, Robert Morris Papers, and George Washington Papers in the Library of Congress. Two indispensable printed primary sources were *The Public Records of the Colony of Connecticut,* I–XV (Hartford, 1850–1890), and *The Public Records of the State of Connecticut,* I–IV (Hartford, 1894–1942). Jared Eliot, *Essays on Field Husbandry* (1752) provided important data on Connecticut agriculture in the mid-eighteenth century. Many of George Washington's wartime letters to Governor Jonathan Trumbull, Sr., were found in John Clement Fitzpatrick, editor, *The Writings of George Washington from the Original Sources, 1745–1799* (Thirty-nine volumes, Washington, D.C., 1931–1944).

The most detailed secondary work, the author's *Jeremiah Wadsworth, Unknown Patriot* (   ), in manuscript when this essay was written, has been drawn upon largely in the description of the administration of the Commissary and Commissary of Purchases departments. The author's "Colonel Henry Champion, Revolutionary Commissary," *Connecticut Historical Society Bulletin,* XXXVI (April, 1971), 52–64, provided data upon Connecticut's role in the interstate system of specific supplies that supported the Continental Army during 1780–1781. Indispensable data for the development of commercial agriculture in the colony of Connecticut and its relation to trade was found in Richard L. Bushman, *From Puritan to Yankee* (Cambridge, 1967), and two unpublished doctoral dissertations, Albert E. Van Dusen, "The Trade of Revolutionary Connecticut" (University of Pennsylvania, 1956), and Gaspare John Saladino, "The Economic Revolution in Late Eighteenth Century Connecticut" (University of Wisconsin, 1964). These two dissertations also supplied important details on Connecticut's wartime economy and the state's role as a major supplier of the Continental Army. Albert E. Van Dusen, *Connecticut* (New York, 1961), was the indispensable general reference. Glenn Weaver, "Industry in an Agrarian Economy," *Connecticut Historical Society Bulletin,* XIX (July, 1964), 82–92, provided insight into the interrelation of agriculture and industry in colonial Connecticut, particularly in the meat packing industry. The early career of a prominent early meat packer is ably presented in Glenn Weaver, *Jonathan Trumbull, Connecticut's Merchant Magistrate* (Hartford, 1956), which provided also a few details on Trumbull's wartime administration. Insight into the relation of George Washington to Governor Trumbull is provided by Douglas Southall Freeman,

George Washington, III–V (New York, 1951–1952). James Truslow Adams, *New England in the Republic, 1776–1850* (Boston, 1926), provides important regional background data for the war years.

Much of the material for this essay was derived from research on Jeremiah Wadsworth under a grant from the American Philosophical Society.